Daily GRAMS® Student Workbook Grade 7

Daily Grams: Guided Review Aiding Mastery Skills®

Author: Dr. Wanda C. Phillips

Easy Grammar Systems®

P.O. Box 25970

Scottsdale, AZ 85255

www.easygrammar.com

©2003

DAILY GRAMS STUDENT WORKBOOK – Grade 7 may not be reproduced. Permission is not granted for district-wide, school-wide, or system-wide use. Reproduction for any commercial use is strictly forbidden. Copyrighted material. All rights reserved. No part of this book may be reproduced, stored in any retrieval system, or transmitted in any form or by any means electronic, mechanical, digital, recording, or otherwise.

DAY 1

CAPITALIZATION:

1. cable cars were used on cottage street in chicago in the 1890's.

PUNCTUATION:

2. Madisons first birthday party was held at noon on January 6 2000

PARTS OF SPEECH: VERBS
Circle the correct form:

3. A. This letter was (wrote, written) by Abraham Lincoln.
   B. Have you ever (drunk, drank) sasparilla?
   C. Your soap (sunk, sank) to the bottom of the pail.
   D. The batter must have been (threw, thrown) a curve ball.
   E. Our balloons had (busted, burst).

PARTS OF SPEECH: ADVERBS/ADJECTIVES
Circle the correct word:

4. For a beginner, Ama twirls her baton (good, well).

SENTENCE COMBINING:

5. Lee is from Korea.
   Lee is an exchange student.
   Lee enjoys horseback riding.

_____

_____

DAY 2

CAPITALIZATION:

1. does mrs. debra c. kirk live on duchess court in muskegon, illinois?

PUNCTUATION:

2. The R D Mann Co has several stores in Phoenix Arizona

PARTS OF SPEECH: NOUNS

Write **C** if the noun is common and **P** if the noun is proper:

3. A. ____ BIRD C. ____ SEARS E. ____ CROW
   B. ____ EGYPT D. ____ MARSH F. ____ GOVERNOR

PARTS OF SPEECH: PRONOUNS

Circle the correct word:

Hint: *If there is a compound pronoun, try placing your finger over the first part. This often helps to determine the correct usage. In other words, place your finger over* Jana and *in the following sentence.*

4. Jana and (she, her) may be hiking the Grand Canyon in May.

SENTENCE COMBINING:

5. Mrs. Hernandez studied the flight plan.
   Mrs. Hernandez walked to her jet.
   Mrs. Hernandez took off.

   _____

   _____

DAY 3

CAPITALIZATION:

1. last spring, they visited craigdarroch castle in victoria, british columbia.

PUNCTUATION:
Punctuate these types of sentences:

2. A. A scorpion stung me   (exclamatory sentence)
   B. Does your brother play tennis   (interrogative sentence)
   C. Hand me your paper   (imperative)
   D. Miguel lifts weights   (declarative)

ANALOGIES:
Analogies make comparisons. First, determine how the first words of an analogy are related (alike, opposite, part of a whole, etc.). After determining the relationship of the first two words (set), look at the third word and the answers. The third word and your answer must show the same relationship as the first two words.

Write the correct letter and word in the space provided:

3. Grape is to raisin as plum is to _____.
   (a) fig   (b) date   (c) drink   (d) prune

   An analogy may also be written in this way:
   Grape : raisin :: plum : _____.
   (a) fig   (b) date   (c) drink   (d) prune

PARTS OF SPEECH: ADVERBS
Circle any adverbs that tell *how*:

4. Those toddlers play well together.

SENTENCE COMBINING:

5. Loni stood at her computer.
   She clicked on her email.

   _____

   _____

DAY 4

CAPITALIZATION:

1. she eats alaskan king crab at maxim restaurant every friday.

PUNCTUATION:

Write the abbreviation for each day of the week:

2. A. Sunday - _____   E. Thursday - _____

   B. Monday - _____   F. Friday - _____

   C. Tuesday - _____   G. Saturday - _____

   D. Wednesday - _____

PARTS OF SPEECH: VERBS

Circle the correct verb:

3. One of the camp leaders (tell, tells) funny stories.

PARTS OF SPEECH: PRONOUNS

Circle the correct compound:

4. (Me and Mick, Mick and me, Mick and I) like crab cakes.

SENTENCE COMBINING:

5. The cottage is painted pink.
   It has blue shutters.
   It is for lease.

   _____

   _____

DAY 5

CAPITALIZATION:

1. the poe family spends memorial day weekend at loganberry campground near mountain trust bank.

PUNCTUATION:

2. Mother Mrs Williams Barbara and I have joined the YWCA

PHRASES/CLAUSES:
A phrase is a group of words.
    Examples: **from me**   **to watch birds**
               sitting on a bench   **trimmed neatly**

A clause contains a subject and a verb (verb phrase).
    Examples: **Licorice tastes good.**
               If you will follow me

Write P if the group of words is a phrase; write C if the group of words is a clause:

3. A. ____ Whenever he laughs   C. ____ The miner removed his hat.
   B. ____ Biting her nails   D. ____ under the truck

PARTS OF SPEECH: VERBS
Unscramble these 23 helping verbs:

4. od -   ash-   yma-   doucl-   nac-   si-   reew-
   ddi-   dha-   gitmh- doulw- liwl- ma- eb-
   sode- vahe- stum-   doushl- laslh- rea- gebin-
                                                  aws-   nebe-

SENTENCE COMBINING:

5. The customer apologized to the clerk.
   The customer was still angry.

_____

_____

DAY 6

CAPITALIZATION:

1. we camped at springbrook state park on lake panorama in iowa.

PUNCTUATION:
Punctuate this address:

2. Mr A Briggs
   12745 N Progress Dr
   Front Royal VA   22630

PREFIXES/ROOTS/SUFFIXES:
A prefix is part of a word that is placed before a root (base) word.
Pre is a prefix that means before.
Pseudo is a prefix that means false.

3. A. Is a preface found at the beginning, middle, or end of a book? _____

   B. The root *nym* means name. What is a pseudonym? _____

PARTS OF SPEECH: NOUNS
Most nouns form the plural (more than one) by adding **s**.

Write **yes** if the word forms the plural by adding **s**; write **no** if it does not:

4. A. _____ braid   C. _____ man   E. _____ parade   G. _____ tremor

   B. _____ flame   D. _____ patio F. _____ goose   H. _____ clasp

SENTENCE COMBINING:

5. An African elephant has large ears.
   An Asian elephant has small ears.

   _____

   _____

DAY 7

CAPITALIZATION:

1. you will enjoy studying the revolutionary war in mr. yardmayer's american history class, phil.

PUNCTUATION:

Punctuate this outline:

2.   I Drop cookies
      A Chocolate chip
      B Lemon drops
  II Roll cookies
      A Snickerdoodles
      B Peanut butter

DICTIONARY: ALPHABETIZING

Write these words in alphabetical order:

    ulcer   spacious   theme   spackle   urban   theater

3. _____

PARTS OF SPEECH: ADJECTIVES

Adjectives are usually describing words.

Circle any descriptive adjectives in the following sentence:

4. Red oily rags lay under the grimy, abandoned van.

SENTENCE COMBINING:

5. Jackson is heavier than Stimpy.
Jackson is lazier than Stimpy.
Jackson and Stimpy are cats.

_____

_____

DAY 8

CAPITALIZATION:

1. in geography class, i did a report on bombay, india, on the arabian sea.

PUNCTUATION:

2. Leela Im loaning you twenty four dollars

PARTS OF SPEECH: INTERJECTIONS

An interjection is a word or phrase (group of words) that expresses emotion.

Circle any interjections:

3. Great! My five dollar bill just flew out the window!

PARTS OF SPEECH: PRONOUNS

Nominative pronouns are *I, he, she, we, they, who, you,* and *it.* Nominative pronouns serve as the subject of a sentence.

Circle the correct pronoun:

4. A. Marco and (her, she) laughed about the comic strip.
   B. Did Brad, Janny, and (he, him) stay at the concert?

SENTENCE COMBINING:

5. The first color television show was produced in 1951.
   Have you ever seen it?

_____

_____

DAY 9

CAPITALIZATION:

1. "when was john kyle elected to the united states senate?" asked trena.

PUNCTUATION:

Write the abbreviation for these months:

2. A. January - _____ E. September - _____

   B. February - _____ F. October - _____

   C. March - _____ G. November - _____

   D. August - _____ H. December - _____

PARTS OF SPEECH:

Circle the correct word:

3. "Lucy doesn't know (anything, nothing) about that," said Alita.

PARTS OF SPEECH: VERBS

Write <u>R</u> if the verb is regular; write <u>IR</u> if the verb is irregular:

4. A. _____ to say   C. _____ to recover   E. _____ to thrill

   B. _____ to ascend   D. _____ to freeze   F. _____ to deny

SENTENCE COMBINING:

5. Patsy mowed their lawn.
   Jonah trimmed grass along a stone fence.

   _____

   _____

DAY 10

CAPITALIZATION:

1. pastor dell of a local lutheran church is of cajun descent, but he doesn't speak french.

PUNCTUATION:

2. Dr Porter my grandmothers neighbor is a veterinarian

PARTS OF SPEECH: VERBS
Underline the subject once and the compound verb twice:

3. The flagwoman lifted her hand and waved drivers forward.

SPELLING:
Most one-syllable words that end in vowel-consonant-consonant, (VCC), do not change when adding a suffix (ending).
   Examples: **bark** + ed = barked   **luck** + y = lucky
                    vent + ing = venting   **sign** + er = signer

4.   A. Add *ful* to wish: _____   C. Add *y* to bulk: _____

     B. Add *ern* to east: _____   D. Add *ing* to bring: _____

SENTENCE COMBINING:

5. Gina looked at her reflection in the mirror.
   She frowned.
   She recombed her hair.

   _____

   _____

DAY 11

CAPITALIZATION:

1. the republican party selected governor dewey of new york as their candidate in 1948.

PUNCTUATION:

2. Lets leave at 9 30 A M on Tuesday said Craig

PARTS OF SPEECH: VERBS

Linking verbs serve to link the subject and a specific noun or adjective in the predicate (verb and words following it). There are 12 commonly used linking verbs.

Unscramble these linking verbs:

3. A. (to) elfe - _____ E. (to) ysat - _____ I. (to) bceemo - _____
   B. (to) etsat - _____ F. (to) emse - _____ J. (to) pearpa - _____
   C. (to) oklo - _____ G. (to) nudos - _____ K. (to) inerma - _____
   D. (to) lemls - _____ H. (to) worg - _____ L. (to) eb - _____

PARTS OF SPEECH: PRONOUNS
Circle the correct pronoun:

4. (Who, Whom) is your favorite cousin?

SENTENCE COMBINING:

5. The forest is heavily wooded.
   It is difficult to walk through it.

_____

_____

DAY 12

CAPITALIZATION:

1. at dinner last monday, jill spread preppy* peanut butter on her steak.
*brand name

PUNCTUATION:

2. Wow   Hes already eaten one fourth cup of hot salsa on three chips

PARTS OF SPEECH: PRONOUNS
Write the possessive pronouns:

3. A. m _ , m _ _ _   D. y _ _ _ , y _ _ _ _   G. t _ _ _ _ , t _ _ _ _ _ _
   B. h _ _   E. i _ _   H. w _ _ _ _
   C. h _ _ , h _ _ _   F. o _ _ , o _ _ _

PARTS OF SPEECH: VERBS
Tense means time.
   Present: Aren **cooks** for his parents.
      Past: Aren **cooked** steak and eggs for his parents.
    Future: Aren **will cook** brunch next Saturday.

Write the tense:

4. A. _____ He **will play** polo next weekend.
   B. _____ A spitz puppy **played** with a chew bone.
   C. _____ Their neighbor **plays** the sitar.

SENTENCE COMBINING:

5. Mack is handing out programs at the band concert.
   Tama is also handing out programs at the band concert.

   _____

   _____

DAY 13

CAPITALIZATION:

1. have you been to wade municipal stadium in duluth, minnesota?

PUNCTUATION:

2. Yes her gardeners club luncheon was postponed until Tuesday April 6

PARTS OF SPEECH: PRONOUNS

Circle the correct word:

Hint: *If there is a compound pronoun, try placing your finger over the first part. This often helps to determine the correct usage. In other words, place your finger over* <u>Miss Parker and</u> *in the following sentence.*

3. Would you like to go with Miss Parker and (I, me)?

PARTS OF SPEECH: ADJECTIVES

A predicate adjective is a describing word that occurs after the verb and describes the subject of the sentence.
                                                                  P.A.
Example: My aunt's wedding <u>gown</u> <u>was</u> *ivory* with delicate pearls.

Underline the subject once and the verb twice. Label the predicate adjective-P.A.:

4. At Thanksgiving, their smoked turkey tasted delicious.

SENTENCE COMBINING:

5. Geese and swans are related.
   Geese are smaller.

_____

_____

DAY 14

CAPITALIZATION:

1. in october, mother always serves boston brown bread and chili for our columbus day dinner.

PUNCTUATION:

2. Martins father in law lives at 22 White Church Road Fairfield PA 17320

PARTS OF SPEECH: ADVERBS

There are seven adverbs that usually tell to what extent. These are <u>not</u>, <u>so</u>, <u>very</u>, <u>too</u>, <u>quite</u>, <u>rather</u>, and <u>somewhat</u>. There are others, but these are the most commonly used.

Circle any adverbs telling *to what extent*:

3. She had not been so foolish as to give her rather unusual opinion about UFO's.

PARTS OF SPEECH: VERBS

Write these contractions:

4. A. should not - _____   D. they will - _____

   B. I have - _____   E. do not - _____

   C. cannot - _____   F. where is - _____

SENTENCE COMBINING:

5. A kumquat is a citrus fruit.
   It is used mainly for preserves.

   _____

   _____

DAY 15

CAPITALIZATION:

1. the patient with alzheimer's disease who has pneumonia was taken to hershey medical center.

PUNCTUATION:

2. We need the following lemons oranges and sun dried apples

PARTS OF SPEECH: VERBS
Circle the verb that agrees with the subject:

3. Nan and her brothers (gather, gathers) berries in the summer.

SENTENCES/FRAGMENTS/RUN-ONS:
A sentence expresses a complete thought.   Example: Use my pen.
A fragment does not express a complete thought.
   Example: Stopped for gas.
A run-on sentence combines too many thoughts or contains a comma splice.
   Examples: I like milk and cookies, but I don't like them in the morning but I try to eat them just before bedtime.
   She ate a cracker, she returned the box to the pantry.

Write S for sentence, F for fragment, and R-O for run-on:

4. A. ____ Luana washed an apple, she offered it to her friend.
   B. ____ He stripped paint from the wood and varnished it.
   C. ____ Last week just before dawn fished for an hour.

SENTENCE COMBINING:

5. An ewer is a vase-shaped pitcher.
   An antique dealer just purchased one.

_____

_____

DAY 16

CAPITALIZATION:

1. do mr. and mrs. little live at 125 river bottom road, norcross, georgia?

PUNCTUATION:

2. Yes his name appeared in our history books index as Rolfe John

DICTIONARY: GUIDE WORDS

Place a √ before a word that will appear on the same dictionary page as the words <u>pelt</u> and <u>pine</u>:

3. A. ___ piece   C. ___ path   E. ___ pink   G. ___ peat

    B. ___ phone   D. ___ please   F. ___ petty   H. ___ pike

PARTS OF SPEECH: VERBS
   An infinitive is *to* + a verb.

4. An example of an infinitive is _____.

SENTENCE COMBINING:

5. Lexa planted peonies in her flower bed.
    Lexa also planted carnations there.
    Lexa planted irises, too.

    _____

    _____

DAY 17

CAPITALIZATION:
Capitalize this outline:

1. i. countries
       a. leaders
       b. types of government
   ii. states
       a. governors
       b. capitols

PUNCTUATION:

2. Kayleigh Martin L P N has worked at Korb Hospital for twenty one years

SPELLING:
Most words that end in *e*, drop the *e* when adding a suffix that begins with a vowel. (The ending *y* is considered a vowel.)
Examples: name + ed = nam<u>ed</u>   releas<u>e</u> + ing = releas<u>ing</u>
             hast<u>e</u> + y = hast<u>y</u>   swindl<u>e</u> + er = swindl<u>er</u>

3. A. Add *y* to ice: _____   C. Add *ing* to tape: _____
   B. Add *ar* to pole: _____   D. Add *able* to receive: _____

PARTS OF SPEECH: PRONOUNS

4. The four demonstrative pronouns all begin with *th*. The demonstrative pronouns are _____, _____, _____, and _____.

SENTENCE COMBINING:

5. A mud puppy is a large American salamander.
   It has bluish black spots.

   _____

   _____

DAY 18

CAPITALIZATION:

1. did the barnett company have a booth at the conference held by the association of independent maryland schools?

PUNCTUATION:

2. William said My name appears on this list as Pride William

PARTS OF SPEECH: VERBS
Select the correct form:

3. A. That shirt must be (shook, shaken) before drying.
   B. Their skates were (stole, stolen) at the rink.
   C. Have you ever (ate, eaten) French fries with vinegar?
   D. She is (setting, sitting) herbs in pots on her window sills.
   E. The dog (sprung, sprang) up on its hind legs.

PARTS OF SPEECH: NOUNS
Circle any nouns:

4. A lemur has a muzzle like a fox, a long tail, and woolly fur.

SENTENCE COMBINING:

5. We went on an outing.
   We ate fried chicken.
   We ate potato salad.
   We ate chili chips.

   _____

   _____

DAY 19

CAPITALIZATION:

1. linda studied english literature, chemistry, and japanese art in college.

PUNCTUATION:

2. Dear Sarah

    Its a beautiful day here in Juneau   Were going to Mt Roberts this afternoon

                                            Your friend
                                            Sally

DIFFICULT WORDS:

Circle the correct word:

3. A. I wonder if (it's, its) going to rain.
   B. Laylah is trying out for the basketball team, (to, two, too).
   C. (There, Their, They're) in a hurry.
   D. Was (your, you're) sweater hand-knitted?

PARTS OF SPEECH: CONJUNCTIONS

4. The three coordinating conjunctions are _____, _____, and _____.

SENTENCE COMBINING:

5. Carli is helping a neighbor to move into his new home.
   Carli is unpacking dishes.
   Carli is washing dishes.

_____

_____

DAY 20

CAPITALIZATION:

Capitalize this friendly letter:

1.
                                          74 north grand view drive

                                          lansing, mi   48906

                                          july 31, 20--

dear koko,

    i enjoyed my stay with you. let's get together for flag day next september. we could meet in lake tahoe, nevada, if you want.

                                          love,
                                          jenny

PUNCTUATION:

2. A weary frowning motorist stood by her broken down car a new Jaguar

DIRECT OBJECTS:
Underline the subject once and the verb or verb phrase twice; label the direct object - <u>D.O.</u>:

3. Nicki hadn't noticed the snake in a pile of brush.

PARTS OF SPEECH: ADJECTIVES/ADVERBS
Circle the correct word:

4. Aunt Cindy is a (good, well) trail guide who rides a horse (good, well).

SENTENCE COMBINING:

5. Carson grabbed his jacket.
    He ran out the door.

_____

_____

DAY 21

CAPITALIZATION:

1. oconer national forest is near lake sinclair just north of macon, georgia.

PUNCTUATION:

2. Dillons new address is 3 N Warren Avenue Oklahoma City Oklahoma 73112

ANTONYMS/SYNONYMS/HOMONYMS:
   Antonyms are words with opposite meanings.
   Synonyms are words with similar meanings.
   Homonyms are words that are spelled differently but sound alike.

3. A. An antonym for shallow is _____.
   B. A synonym for sharp is _____.
   C. A homonym for shear is _____.

PARTS OF SPEECH: PRONOUNS
   Objective pronouns are *me, him, her, us, them, whom, it,* and *you*.
   Objective pronouns serve as an object.
   Examples: His dad hugged **him**.   **direct object**
                    They sent **her** a raft.   **indirect object,**
                    Come with **me**.   **object of the preposition**

   Circle the correct pronoun:

4. Follow (we, us).

SENTENCE COMBINING:

5. A workshop on self-defense will be held.
   It will start at nine.
   It will be held at a local library.
   It will be free.

_____

_____

DAY 22

CAPITALIZATION:

1. they played chinese checkers while watching an old <u>leave it to beaver</u> show.

PUNCTUATION:

2. Molly Arnes CPA has worked in Virginia since she graduated in 94

PARTS OF SPEECH: VERBS
   Linking verbs serve to link the subject and a specific noun or adjective in the predicate. They do not show action.

   Place an <u>X</u> in the box if the verb is a possible linking verb:

3. A. ___ to feel   D. ___ to be   G. ___ to grow
   B. ___ to deliver   E. ___ to taste   H. ___ to smell
   C. ___ to appear   F. ___ to touch   I. ___ to look

PHRASES/CLAUSES:
   A phrase is two or more words; it does not contain subject and verb.
   A clause contains a subject and a verb.

   Write <u>P</u> if the group of words is a phrase; write <u>C</u> if the group of words is a clause:

4. A. ____ When Pablo was a baby
   B. ____ Without a seatbelt
   C. ____ Sending an email

SENTENCE COMBINING:

5. A shofar is a ram's-horn trumpet.
   It was blown by ancient Hebrews in battle.

   _____

   _____

DAY 23

CAPITALIZATION:

1. is the great pyramid in an african desert near the gulf of suez?

PUNCTUATION:

2. Miss James the biology teacher listed the following rules

   A Rule 1   No tardies
   B Rule 2   Bathroom passes for emergencies only

ANALOGIES:
Analogies make comparisons. First, determine how the first words of an analogy are related (alike, opposite, part of a whole, etc.) After determining the relationship of the first two words, look at the third word and the answers. The third word and your answer must show the same relationship as the first two words.

Complete this analogy:

3. decay : rot :: lethal : _____
   (a) gaseous   (b) daring   (c) deadly   (d) brave

PARTS OF SPEECH: ADJECTIVES
Circle the correct adjective form:

4. The singer appeared (nervouser, more nervous) during her second song.

SENTENCE COMBINING:

5. Periwinkle can be a flowering ground cover.
   Periwinkle can also refer to a kind of marine snail.

   _____

   _____

DAY 24

CAPITALIZATION:

1. lisa sipped her grisko's* coffee as she wrote to the u. s. department of interior about her concern for endangered birds.

*brand name

PUNCTUATION:

2. The y in your last name is illegible remarked Patrick

PARTS OF SPEECH: NOUNS

Nouns ending in <u>sh</u>, <u>ch</u>, <u>s</u>, <u>x</u>, and <u>z</u> usually add <u>es</u> to form the plural (more than one).

Write a singular noun and its plural for a word ending in the following:

	singular noun	plural noun
3. A. sh -	_____	_____
B. ch -	_____	_____
C. s -	_____	_____
D. x -	_____	_____
E. z -	_____	_____

PARTS OF SPEECH: PRONOUNS

Circle the correct pronoun:

4. "Would you like to go with Lenny and (I, me)?" asked Rob.

SENTENCE COMBINING:

5. The emergency operator answered the telephone.
   He heard only a dial tone.

   _____

   _____

DAY 25

CAPITALIZATION:

1. "did wilt chamberlain play for the harlem globe trotters?" inquired liz.

PUNCTUATION:

2. Yeah Weve won a vacation to the beautiful sunny island of Crete

PARTS OF SPEECH: ADVERBS
   Adverbs tell *where*.
   Write five adverbs that tell where you might go:

3. _____, _____, _____,

   _____, and _____

PARTS OF SPEECH: NOUNS
   Write the possessive form:

4. A. a CD belonging to Vince - _____

   B. a reception for Carol and Dave - _____

   C. equipment belonging to scuba divers - _____

   D. hiking gear belonging to Chris - _____

SENTENCE COMBINING:

5. In 1907, women in the United States had not won the right to vote.
   Women in Finland had.

   _____

   _____

DAY 26

CAPITALIZATION:

1. my friend, juan, attends a hispanic fair each year to celebrate cinco de mayo*.
*name of a special day

PUNCTUATION:

2. They announced their engagement on Saturday October 19 1999

PARTS OF SPEECH: VERBS
List the 23 helping verbs:

3. d____ h____ m____ ____ould c____ i____ w____
   d____ h____ m____ ____ould w____ a____ b____
   d____ h____ m____ ____ould s____ a____ b____
                                  w____   b____

TEXT COMPONENTS:

4. A. At the beginning of a book, the _____ provides a listing of chapters and tells to which page to turn to find each chapter.

   B. The date a book was published is usually found on the title page or on the back of the title page. This date is called the _____.

SENTENCE COMBINING:

5. The company closed its animation studio.
   Profits had decreased.

   _____
   _____

DAY 27

CAPITALIZATION:

1. his father teaches german, math, and biology I at pioneer high school.

PUNCTUATION:

Punctuate the heading and salutation of this friendly letter:

2.　　　　　　　　　　　　　　　　　　　　　　　94705 Mansfield Rd
　　　　　　　　　　　　　　　　　　　　　　　　Shreveport LA   71118
　　　　　　　　　　　　　　　　　　　　　　　　April 12 20--

　　Dear Amba

PARTS OF SPEECH: ADVERBS

Circle any adverbs that tells *when*:

3. Yesterday, our math class seemed to last forever.

INDIRECT OBJECT:

Underline the subject once and the verb or verb phrase twice. Label the direct object - D.O. and the indirect object - I.O.:

4. The delivery person gave my brother three small packages.

SENTENCE COMBINING:

5. April became a naval architect.
　　She took her first job in Chicago.
　　She designs ships.

_____

_____

DAY 28

CAPITALIZATION:
Capitalize these titles:

1. A. night flying
   B. "the case of the laughing butler"
   C. staying healthy with nutrition

PUNCTUATION:

2. On July 20 1969 the Apollo astronauts walked on the moon

PHRASES/CLAUSES:
A phrase is a group of words.
   Examples: toward the west   to see you
              having gasped   burned and blistered

A clause contains a subject and a verb (verb phrase).
   Examples: <u>Snow</u> <u>blanketed</u> the forest.
              When <u>they</u> <u>went</u> to the beach

Write <u>P</u> if the group of words is a phrase; write <u>C</u> if the group of words is a clause:

3. A. ____ To bring good news   C. ____ Leaving early in the morning
   B. ____ Although the urn was old D. ____ Fried to a crisp

PARTS OF SPEECH: ADVERBS/ADJECTIVES
Circle the correct word:

4. Jack said that he doesn't feel (good, well).

SENTENCE COMBINING:

5. Miss Littel is a fashion designer.
   Before that, she was a first grade teacher.

_____

_____

DAY 29

CAPITALIZATION:

1. the progressive party candidate in 1924 was robert m. la follette.

PUNCTUATION:

2. Have Tori Trevor and Matty seen your pretty lighted tree

DICTIONARY USAGE:

 elephantine (e-le-fan-tēn) adj. 1 *a*: having enormous size or strength *b*: clumsy, ponderous 2: of or pertaining to an elephant

Use this entry to answer the following questions:

3. A. How many syllables are in *elephantine*? _____
  B. Does the final syllablle rhyme with mine, bed, or seen? _____
  C. There are eight parts of speech: noun *(n.)*, adjective *(adj.)*, verb *(v.)*, adverb *(adv.)*, pronoun *(pro.)*, preposition *(prep.)*, conjunction *(conj.)*, and interjection *(intj.)*.
   What part of speech is *elephantine*? _____
  D. His *elephantine* muscles gleamed as he lifted the heavy weights.
   Which meaning, 1a, 1b, or 2, applies to *elephantine* as it is used in the above sentence? _____

PARTS OF SPEECH: INTERJECTIONS
 Circle any interjections:

4. This pork chop tastes rancid! Yuck!

SENTENCE COMBINING:

5. Mrs. Anders traveled to Vienna.
 She purchased Austrian crystal pins.
 The pins were gifts for her friends.

_____

_____

DAY 30

CAPITALIZATION:

1. "jana and i made indian fry bread to sell at birk elementary school's bake sale last march," said brad.

PUNCTUATION:
  Punctuate these types of sentences:

2. A. She encountered a wild boar while walking   (declarative sentence)
   B. Where is Tombstone   (interrogative sentence)
   C. Take this, please   (imperative sentence)
   D. Your sculpture won first place in the art contest   (exclamatory sentence)

PARTS OF SPEECH: PRONOUNS
  Circle the correct pronoun:

3. Tugging hard on the rope, Craig exclaimed, "(We, Us) kids don't have a chance!"

PARTS OF SPEECH: NOUNS
  Write **A** if the noun is abstract and **C** if the noun is concrete:

4. A. ____ puppet   C. ____ pasta   E. ____ pride
   B. ____ peace   D. ____ purity   F. ____ perch

SENTENCE COMBINING:

5. An inky cap is a type of mushroom.
   It emits an inky fluid after maturing.

   _____

   _____

DAY 31

CAPITALIZATION:

1. the shinto religion, i think, is a major religion in japan.

PUNCTUATION:

2. No we wont be arriving in Denver Colorado until 2 30

LIBRARY SKILLS:

Place an X before each true statement:

3. A. _____ Nonfiction books are true.
   B. _____ A book about the habitat of a turtle is a type of nonfiction book.
   C. _____ Nonfiction books have a call number.
   D. _____ Nonfiction books tell a created story.

PARTS OF SPEECH: VERBS

To sit means to rest.
To set means to place.   You must have an object to place; this is called a direct object.

Circle the correct verb. With a form of *to set*, label the direct object - D.O.:

4. A. He (sat, set) the iron on his bathroom floor.
   B. Mrs. Zee (sat, set) with her head tilted, listening intently to the speech.

SENTENCE COMBINING:

5. The athlete hurt her leg.
   The MRI revealed swelling.
   The MRI did not show a broken bone.

   _____

   _____

DAY 32

CAPITALIZATION:

1. is mt. st. mary's college in maryland considered to be in the south?

PUNCTUATION:

2. She adjusted the purses zipper but it still wouldnt close

DICTIONARY: ALPHABETIZING
Write these words in alphabetical order:
gravid   entail   fourth   frame   jawbone   forth

3. _____

PARTS OF SPEECH: NOUNS
Write **C** if the noun is common and **P** if the noun is proper:

4. A. ____ CINDY   C. ____ CITY   E. ____ MT. BALDY
   B. ____ STYLIST   D. ____ DETROIT   F. ____ IDAHO

SENTENCE COMBINING:

5. A muntjac is a small deer of southeastern Asia.
   It also lives in the East Indies.
   It is also called a barking deer.

   _____

   _____

DAY 33

CAPITALIZATION:

1. on monday, september 17, they embarked on the <u>duchess regal</u> for an alaskan cruise.

PUNCTUATION:

2. Miss Ving likes to read and drink hot chocolate on cold snowy days

PARTS OF SPEECH: VERBS

To rise means to go up (without help).
To raise means to go up (with help). An object needs to be raised; this is called a direct object.

Circle the correct verb. With a form of *to raise*, label the direct object - D.O.:

3. A. Bread (rises, raises) due to yeast.
   B. The guard (rose, raised) his hand in protest.

DICTIONARY SKILLS:

A syllable is a unit of sound.

Write the number of syllables in each word:

4. A. _____ bubble   C. _____ exhibition   E. _____ gradual
   B. _____ regular   D. _____ screenwriter   F. _____ chrome

SENTENCE COMBINING:

5. Carl lifted the crying infant.
   The baby began to coo.

_____

_____

DAY 34

CAPITALIZATION:

1. salt point is in chippewa county on whitefish bay, michigan.

PUNCTUATION:

2. Mr Jamison was surprised by our gift a ticket to a hockey game

PREFIXES/ROOTS/SUFFIXES:

A root is defined as a simple element from which a word is derived. A root may form a word as in *cook* or it may not stand alone as a word as in *vis*.

The root *dict* means *to say*.

3. A. What does predict mean? _____

   B. How does dictionary relate to the meaning of *dict*? _____
   _____

PARTS OF SPEECH: VERBS
 Write these contractions:

4. A. I shall - _____   D. has not - _____

   B. she is - _____   E. we will - _____

   C. will not - _____   F. could not - _____

SENTENCE COMBINING:

5. The defensive tackle signed a contract.
   It was for one year.
   It was for slightly over a million dollars.

   _____

   _____

DAY 35

CAPITALIZATION:

1. tara and her mother attend the fountain hills art show each year.

PUNCTUATION:

2. By the way we need the following for our party balloons favors and crepe paper

PARTS OF SPEECH: NOUNS
   Write the possessive form:

3. A. the sense of humor of Ricky - _____

   B. an office shared by two women - _____

   C. a sailboat owned by their aunts - _____

   D. a space suit belonging to an astronaut - _____

PARTS OF SPEECH: VERBS

4. An example of an infinitive is _____.

SENTENCE COMBINING:

5. The panther's eyes glowed.
   He growled.
   He pounced.

_____

_____

DAY 36

CAPITALIZATION:

1. his grandfather visited nancy hanks memorial in the appalachian mountains of west virginia.

PUNCTUATION:

2. Bill please come in watch television and wait for me

PARTS OF SPEECH: VERBS

To lie means to rest.
To lay means to place.   You place an object; this is called a direct object.   <u>Important</u>: With *lays, laying,* and *laid,* look for a direct object.

Circle the correct verb. With a form of *to lay,* label the direct object - **D.O.**:

3. A. Their hamster is (lying, laying) at the bottom of the cage.
    B. The majorette had (laid, lain) her baton on the ground.
    C. We must have (laid, lain) in the sun too long.

PARTS OF SPEECH: PREPOSITIONS

Circle any preposition:

4. again   against   toward   within   twice   on   behind   together
    around   after   tonight   when   to   in   belong   along

SENTENCE COMBINING:

5. A male duck is called a drake.
    A male goose is called a gander.

_____

_____

DAY 37

CAPITALIZATION:

1. yesterday, the american red cross sent supplies to turkey.

PUNCTUATION:
Punctuate these titles:

2. A. Walk Two Moons   (book)
    B. Custom Pieces   (magazine article)
    C. The Skaters' Waltz   (song)
    D. October Sky   (movie)
    E. John Henry   (poem)

PARTS OF SPEECH: ADJECTIVES
Circle the correct form:

3. Oliver and Olivia are twins; his hair is (darker, darkest).

PARTS OF SPEECH: VERBS
Circle the correct verb:

4. A. The model has (brought, brung) his portfolio today.
    B. That chef must have already (took, taken) the dessert from the oven.
    C. Their friends may have (went, gone) to the horse show.

SENTENCE COMBINING:

5. The speaker has charm.
    The speaker has wit.
    The speaker is intelligent.
    My uncle is the speaker.

    _____

    _____

DAY 38

CAPITALIZATION:

1. we traveled south on interstate 26 to reach the westgate mall in spartansburg, south carolina.

PUNCTUATION:

2. Whenever Barts parents camp they search for a small secluded stream

PARTS OF SPEECH: VERBS

3. Five irregular verbs are _____, _____, _____, _____, and _____.

SPELLING:

Most one-syllable words that end in consonant-vowel-consonant, (CVC), double the final letter when adding a suffix (ending) that begins with a vowel. (The ending *y* is considered a vowel.)

Examples: **brim** + ed = bri<u>mm</u>ed   **stop** + ing = sto<u>pp</u>ing
            rub + ing = ru<u>bb</u>ing   crab + y = cra<u>bb</u>y

4. A. Add *ed* to star: _____   C. Add *y* to slop: _____

    B. Add *er* to drum: _____   D. Add *ing* to nag: _____

SENTENCE COMBINING:

5. An ermine's coat usually becomes white in winter.
    The tip of its tail remains black.

_____

_____

DAY 39

CAPITALIZATION:

1. for grandma's birthday gift, cory and i bought an ontari blender from zerfing's appliance store.

PUNCTUATION:

2. Logan announced Weve decided to marry on December 27 2022 at 2 oclock

PARTS OF SPEECH: ADVERBS
Circle the correct word:

3. "Don't get (no, any) big ideas about throwing mud," scolded her sister.

SENTENCES/FRAGMENTS/RUN-ONS:

A sentence expresses a complete thought.   Example: I enjoy music.

A fragment does not express a complete thought.
Example: Before the second inning went to buy a drink.

A run-on sentence combines too many thoughts or contains a comma splice.
Examples: The book was interesting and about two sailors caught in a storm but they were rescued and went to Spain.
He burned finger, he placed it under running water.

Write S for sentence, F for fragment, and R-O for run-on:

4. A. ____ Her glare told us that she was not happy.
   B. ____ Jana, resting her foot on the brake at a traffic light.
   C. ____ They moved, all of their friends helped them.

SENTENCE COMBINING:

5. Lang enjoyed his hiking trip.
   Lang got blisters on his heels.

   _____

   _____

DAY 40

CAPITALIZATION:

1. the town of red shirt is near badlands national park in south dakota.

PUNCTUATION:

2. Mrs Henry shouldnt speak she has laryngitis

PARTS OF SPEECH: VERBS
   Underline the verb or verb phrase twice:

3. A. Our mail has (come, came) early.
   B. You should have (saw, seen) his expression.
   C. The witness had (swore, sworn) to tell the truth.
   D. Carlotta had been (chosen, chose) as one of the finalists.
   E. It (began, begun) to drizzle during the evening.

PARTS OF SPEECH: PREPOSITIONS
   Circle the prepositional phrase. Box the object of the preposition:

4. The beachcomber sat against a tall palm tree.

SENTENCE COMBINING:

5. Italians celebrate Easter by baking bread.
   The bread has eggs in it.
   The eggs are whole.
   The eggs are hard-boiled.

   _____

   _____

DAY 41

CAPITALIZATION:

1. each autumn, aunt jane sells her crafts at the apple harvest festival held at south mountain.

PUNCTUATION:

2. Miki has been elected class vice president and youre the secretary   said Ms Ort

DICTIONARY: GUIDE WORDS

Place a √ before a word that will appear on the same dictionary page as the words <u>troll</u> and <u>tuck</u>:

3. A. ___ tubular   C. ___ trick   E. ___ truck   G. ___ truthful

    B. ___ tryst   D. ___ tsar   F. ___ Tuesday   H. ___ tucket

PARTS OF SPEECH: CONJUNCTIONS

4. Write a sentence containing two coordinating conjunctions. Circle them.

   _____

   _____

SENTENCE COMBINING:

5. A baleen whale is also called a fin whale.
   It can be found in arctic waters.
   It can be found in tropical waters.

   _____

   _____

DAY 42

CAPITALIZATION:

1. the governor will vote at a presbyterian church on east happy valley road next tuesday.

PUNCTUATION:
Punctuate this address:

2. _____

   _____

   _____

              Mrs Anka R Brown
              495992 S Sheridan St
              Las Vegas NV   89102

FRIENDLY LETTERS/ENVELOPES:
Write your return address on the lines in number 2:

3. Do not use abbreviations except for your state's postal code.

PARTS OF SPEECH: VERBS
Circle the verb that agrees with the subject:

4. People (need, needs) to keep streams clear of debris.

SENTENCE COMBINING:

5. Marco asked his boss for a raise.
   Marco pointed out his major accomplishments.

   _____

   _____

DAY 43

CAPITALIZATION:

1. the lott family attended the olympics held in atlanta, georgia.

PUNCTUATION:

Write the abbreviation:

2. A. mountain - _____   E. meter - _____
   B. December - _____   F. Friday - _____
   C. street - _____   G. March - _____
   D. Tuesday - _____   H. west - _____

PARTS OF SPEECH: ADJECTIVES

Adjectives are usually describing words.

Circle any descriptive adjectives in the following sentence:

3. A heron is a long-necked wading bird with a long, tapering bill and soft feathers.

PARTS OF SPEECH: VERBS

Write the tense:

4. A. _____ I'll ask my grandfather about a main-mast.
   B. _____ They built an alcove off their living room.
   C. _____ Lil researched Alaskan salmon for her report.

SENTENCE COMBINING:

5. Michigan has 124 lighthouses.
   It has more than any other state.

   _____

   _____

DAY 44

CAPITALIZATION:

1. have you told mother that tom l. johnson was the first to use a car in a political campaign?

PUNCTUATION:

2. James S Reese D V S arrived to examine several cows udders

DIFFICULT WORDS:
  Circle the correct word:

3.   A. "(Can, May) I give you some advice?" asked Miss Wing.
     B. "I doubt if (your, you're) aware of the error," remarked Peter.
     C. "A seal wiggled (its, it's) nose at me," said Lulu with a giggle.
     D. "(There, Their, They're) must be an explanation!" exclaimed the lawyer.

PARTS OF SPEECH: PRONOUNS
  Circle any possessive pronouns:

4. Every January, my teacher and her friends sled on a hill near our home.

SENTENCE COMBINING:

5. The okapi is a mammal.
   It is related to the giraffe.
   It lives in Zaire.
   It has a short neck.

_____

_____

DAY 45

CAPITALIZATION:

1. a polynesian surfer gave us directions to sunset beach in oahu*.

*name of an island in Hawaii

PUNCTUATION:

2. After two hours of shopping the womens bags were overflowing and heavy

PREFIXES/ROOTS/SUFFIXES:

A suffix is an ending to a root.

The suffix *ist* means (a) a person who performs a special action, (b) a person who makes or produces a specified thing, (c) one who specializes in a specific art or science, (d) one who has a certain belief, (e) one who plays a specialized instrument, or (f) one who operates a specialized mechanical device.

3. A. To which meaning would <u>cyclist</u> pertain? _____
   B. To which meaning would <u>geologist</u> pertain? _____
   C. To which meaning would <u>socialist</u> pertain? _____

PARTS OF SPEECH: CONJUNCTIONS

Circle the correlative conjunctions:

4. She has taken either her dog or her cat to an animal clinic.

SENTENCE COMBINING:

5. The officials want better salaries.
   They want improved pensions.
   They want increased medical benefits.
   The officials are striking.

   _____

   _____

DAY 46

CAPITALIZATION:

1. a social worker from new york, frances perkins, was the first woman to be appointed to the cabinet*.

*advisory group to the U. S. President

PUNCTUATION:
Punctuate this inside address and salutation of a business letter:

2. The Business Center
   17205 Butherus Way
   Scottsdale Arizona   85267

   Dear Sir

PARTS OF SPEECH: PRONOUNS
Circle any reflexive pronouns:

3. The children played by themselves in the walkway leading to their apartment.

PARTS OF SPEECH: VERBS
Linking verbs do not show action. However, some verbs can serve as an action verb or as a linking verb.
   Hint: In deciding if a verb is action or linking, try placing *is, am, are, was,* or *were* in its place. If it doesn't change the sentence meaning, it's usually linking.
                                  are
         Example: You <u>appear</u> very angry.   (*Appear* is a linking verb here.)
Write <u>LV</u> if the verb is linking and <u>AV</u> if the verb is action:

4. A. ____ She <u>looked</u> into the refrigerator for a snack.
    B. ____ She <u>looks</u> pretty in her new long dress.

SENTENCE COMBINING:

5. Alicia is meeting new clients on Monday morning.
   Alicia has to fly to North Dakota for a conference after that.

   _____

   _____

DAY 47

CAPITALIZATION:

1. is otter creek wayside state park on oregon's pacific coast?

PUNCTUATION:

2. Publilus Syrus a Latin writer said It is only the ignorant who despise education

ANALOGIES:
Complete this analogy:

3. mutton : sheep :: venison : _____
   (a) Venice   (b) beef   (c) deer   (d) wool

PARTS OF SPEECH: NOUNS
Circle any nouns:

4. Gnocchi is a dumpling made of potato or semolina and served with a sauce.

SENTENCE COMBINING:

5. Toby is an organic gardener.
Toby grows his own vegetables.
Toby uses only natural fertilizers.

_____

_____

DAY 48

CAPITALIZATION:

1. during the 1700's, the russian-american fur company set up trading posts in north america.

PUNCTUATION:

2. Yes her loud unusual behavior immediately drew three nurses attention

PARTS OF SPEECH: ADVERBS

Circle any adverbs that tell *where*:

3. Fishing downstream, she watched salmon swim by.

PARTS OF SPEECH: NOUNS

A noun ending in *ay, ey, oy, uy,* and *iy* add <u>s</u> to form the plural.
A singular noun ending in <u>consonant + y</u> (any letter other than *a, e, i, o,* or *u*) changes the <u>y</u> to <u>i</u> and adds <u>es</u>.
        Examples: tr**ay** - tray**s**   gup**py** - gupp**ies**

Write the plural of each noun:

4. A. artery - _____   D. drapery - _____

   B. ruby - _____   E. dray - _____

   C. decoy - _____   F. trolley - _____

SENTENCE COMBINING:

5. A yak is a long-haired oxen.
   Its habitat is Tibet or other high areas of Asia.

_____

_____

DAY 49

CAPITALIZATION:
Capitalize this friendly letter:

1.
                                                354 west deen street
                                                forest city, nc   28043
                                                november 15, 20--

dear ryan,
      thanks for writing letters to our class. liberty middle school sounds great. which subjects do you like? (i like science, civics, and algebra II.)
      i'm an average fifteen year old who likes music. i have a sister, ellen, and a golden retriever named bose.

                                                  your new pen pal,
                                                manzo

PUNCTUATION:

2. His brother in law enlisted in the U S Army on August 14 1998

TEXT COMPONENTS:

3. The _____ is a listing of information and page numbers found at the end of a book.

PARTS OF SPEECH: PRONOUNS
Circle the correct pronoun:

4. Chuck explained, "The last two to leave the cook-out were Jay and (me, I).

SENTENCE COMBINING:

5. The computer chip operates at 1.5 gigahertz.
That is 1.5 billion cycles per second.

_____

_____

DAY 50

CAPITALIZATION:

1. a table, decorated with english tea roses, had been placed in the lobby of north bay inn.

PUNCTUATION:

2. Shopping list
   - ~ twenty four candy bars
   - ~ one gal of milk
   - ~ Mexican style beans

SUBJECT/VERB:
Underline the subject once and the verb or verb phrase twice:

3. During the sudden afternoon storm, several canoeists had rowed quickly to shore.

PARTS OF SPEECH: PRONOUNS
An antecedent is a word to which a possessive pronoun refers.

   Example: The little <u>girl</u> grabbed **her** mitt from the bench.

   Her is a possessive pronoun that modifies (goes over to) *mitt*. However, **her** refers back to the *girl*. *Girl* is the antecedent.

Circle the antecedent of the boldfaced possessive pronoun:

4. Surveying the area below, an eagle sat on **its** perch, a broken branch above the canyon.

SENTENCE COMBINING:

5. That carpenter remodeled his kitchen.
   He added a skylight.
   He built a center island.
   He put granite counter tops on the center island.

_____

_____

DAY 51

CAPITALIZATION:

1. cross memorial bridge near bismarck convention center to get to apple creek golf course.

PUNCTUATION:

2. No planes dont fly to that remote area but you can hike there

DICTIONARY USAGE:

    scion (sī-on) n. 1: a detached living portion of a plant joined to a stock in grafting 2: descendant, child

3. A. Does the first syllablle rhyme with my, me, or mitt? _____
   B. There are eight parts of speech: noun *(n.)*, adjective *(adj.)*, verb *(v.)*, adverb *(adv.)*, pronoun *(pro.)*, preposition *(prep.)*, conjunction *(conj.)*, and interjection *(intj.)*.
      What part of speech is *scion*? _____
   C. What letter is silent in *scion*? _____
   D. That family tradition is best left to a scion.
      Which definition applies to use of *scion* in the above sentence? _____

PARTS OF SPEECH: PREPOSITIONS
Circle any preposition:

4. past   passed   until   from   about   once   behind   underneath
   amid   across   my   for   its   down   beyond   concerning

SENTENCE COMBINING:

5. The tourists traveled by gondola.
   They were visiting Venice, Italy.
   The gondolier sang to the tourists.

_____

_____

DAY 52

CAPITALIZATION:

1. she parked her palo* truck in front of muslim community mosque on frye street.

*brand name

PUNCTUATION:

2. Talented and hard working Benjamin Franklin published Poor Richards Almanac

ANTONYMS/SYNONYMS/HOMONYMS:

Antonyms are words with opposite meanings.
Synonyms are words with similar meanings.
Homonyms are words that are spelled differently but sound alike.

3. A. An antonym for *capture* is _____.
   B. A synonym for *irk* is _____.
   C. A homonym for *prays* is _____.

DIFFICULT WORDS:

Circle the correct word:

4. A. (There, Their, They're) thinking about using a wrench on that pipe.
   B. "(Your, You're) one of the best lacross players," remarked a spectator.
   C. Is that (your, you're) final answer?
   D. This television show is (to, two, too) scary.

SENTENCE COMBINING:

5. Mexico has 756,061 square miles of land.
   This is about three times the size of Texas.

   _____

   _____

DAY 53

CAPITALIZATION:
Capitalize these titles:

1. A. stranger in the forest

   B. music to your ears

   C. "one is a wanderer"

PUNCTUATION:

2. Hes my friend said Regis and Ill wait for his late bus

PHRASES/CLAUSES:
Write P if the group of words is a phrase; write C if the group of words is a clause:

3. A. _____ Unable to see
   B. _____ If I were you
   C. _____ Scott ironed his shirt
   D. _____ Refereeing the basketball game

PARTS OF SPEECH: ADJECTIVES
Circle the correct adjective form:

4. Is butter (healthier, more healthy) than margarine?

SENTENCE COMBINING:

5. There are many types of roofs.
   One type of roof is mansard.
   Two other types of roofs are gambrel and hip.

   _____

   _____

DAY 54

CAPITALIZATION:

1. was president franklin d. roosevelt, a democrat, ever a member of the house of representatives?

PUNCTUATION:

2. A Korat a cat from Thailand has a heart shaped face a silver blue coat and green eyes

PARTS OF SPEECH: ADVERBS

Adverbs tell *when*.

Write four adverbs that tell when you might do homework:

3. _____, _____, _____,
   and _____

SENTENCES/FRAGMENTS/RUN-ONS:
* A sentence expresses a complete thought.
* A fragment does not express a complete thought.
* A run-on sentence combines too many thoughts or contains a comma between two complete thoughts.
   Example: Lightning had struck the forest, a fire burned out of control.

Write S for sentence, F for fragment, and R-O for run-on:

4. A. ____ Wind swept through our picnic area, we grabbed our paper plates.
   B. ____ During auctions, that dealer nods his bids.
   C. ____ Looking to the left for oncoming cars.

SENTENCE COMBINING:

5. The pavement had been made of "granitoid."
   This is a mixture of concrete and chips of granite.

   _____

   _____

DAY 55

CAPITALIZATION:

1. "my mother always makes oriental chicken salad for christmas eve dinner," remarked rick.

PUNCTUATION:

2. Taking her first step the baby grinned wavered and tumbled to the floor

PARTS OF SPEECH: VERBS
   List the 23 helping verbs:

3. _____

   _____

PARTS OF SPEECH: PRONOUNS
   Circle the correct pronoun:

4. To (who, whom) did Anita give her ping pong paddle?

SENTENCE COMBINING:

5. A hansom is a two-wheeled covered carriage.
   The driver's seat is elevated behind the cab.
   It was designed by an English architect.

   _____

   _____

DAY 56

CAPITALIZATION:

1. is howard university in washington, d. c., near the national zoological park?

PUNCTUATION:

2. Mary Davis a member of the Cashtown Ladies Auxiliary made soup sandwiches and pies for the event

DICTIONARY: ALPHABETIZING

Write these words in alphabetical order:

      pica   picante   iris   libel   picadore   kennel

3. _____

PARTS OF SPEECH: VERBS
Circle the correct verb:

4. A. He must have (driven, drove) the back road to Cherry Creek.

   B. Granddad has (blown, blew) up all the balloons for our party.

   C. I might have (gave, given) you the wrong address.

   D. Ice cubes were (froze, frozen) in the shape of watermelon slices.

SENTENCE COMBINING:

5. Misha raised her voice.
   She called to her children.
   They were playing softball.

   _____

   _____

DAY 57

CAPITALIZATION:

1. we picnicked near mt. mansfield in the green mountains of vermont and then drove to lake champlain.

PUNCTUATION:

2. Dads strawberry filled pancakes were light and fluffy but his buttery caramel syrup made them soggy

SENTENCE TYPES:

Write a declarative sentence:

3. _____

PARTS OF SPEECH: NOUNS

A predicate nominative occurs after a linking verb and means the same as the subject. A predicate nominative is often a noun.

  P.N.
Example: Kaleigh is a **clown** for children's parties.

Underline the subject once and the verb twice; label the predicate nominative-P.N.:

4. Mrs. Jones was the church secretary for three years.

SENTENCE COMBINING:

5. Her hair is brown.
   It has blonde streaks in it.
   Her hair is long.
   She usually wears it in a braid.

_____

_____

DAY 58

CAPITALIZATION:

1. "the sarsi indians lived in present day western canada," the teacher said.

PUNCTUATION:

2. Apart from a few up to date appliances the old farmhouse remained unchanged

PARTS OF SPEECH: NOUNS

Write the possessive form:

3. A. a computer that Ellie owns - _____

    B. an apartment shared by two boys - _____

    C. bristles in a toothbrush - _____

LIBRARY SKILLS:

Place an X before each true statement:

4. A. _____ The letters *ju* refer to children's literature.

    B. _____ A fiction book tells a made-up story.

    C. _____ Fiction books are placed alphabetically according to the author's last name.

    D. _____ A biography is the story of a person's life written by the person himself.

SENTENCE COMBINING:

5. Roquefort is a type of cheese.
   It takes its name from a village in France.

   _____

   _____

DAY 59

CAPITALIZATION:

1. during the 1820's, american missionaries went to hawaii to teach people about christianity.

PUNCTUATION:

2. Katie didnt you join the ASA* last January

*Arizona Songwriters' Association

PARTS OF SPEECH: INTERJECTIONS/CONJUNCTIONS
   Circle any interjections; box any conjunctions:

3. Ouch! My index finger and thumb may be sprained!

PREFIXES/ROOTS/SUFFIXES:

   A root is defined as a simple element from which a word is derived.

   The root *dent* comes from a French word meaning *tooth.*

4. A. A dentifrice is a substance for cleaning _____?

   B. Write another word that uses *dent* meaning *tooth.* _____

       What does your word mean? _____

SENTENCE COMBINING:

5. Handprints are done in concrete outside Mann's Chinese Theater.
   Mary Pickford was the first woman.
   The year was 1927.

   _____

   _____

DAY 60

CAPITALIZATION:

1. glasgow international airport in montana is west of fort peck indian reservation.

PUNCTUATION:

2. Nicknamed the City of Roses Portland Oregon has the oldest and largest rose garden in America

PARTS OF SPEECH: NOUNS
Write a propr noun for each common noun:

3. A. team - _____
   B. landmark - _____
   C. corporation - _____

PARTS OF SPEECH: PRONOUNS
A possessive pronoun must agree with the number and gender of the word to which it refers:
   Incorrect: The **man** extended *her* hand to a friend. (gender)
   The **man** extended *their* hand to a friend. (number)
   Correct: The **man** extended *his* hand to a friend.

Circle the correct pronoun:

4. A. Many Civil War soldiers left (their, his) farms to fight.
   B. One of the girls asked to tell about (their, her) early childhood.

SENTENCE COMBINING:

5. Marshall stays with his aunt each summer.
   His aunt lives in Wyoming.
   His aunt lives on a ranch.

   _____

   _____

DAY 61

CAPITALIZATION:

1. "did i tell you," asked michael, "about my college english and history classes?"

PUNCTUATION:
Punctuate these titles:

2. A. Northeast Living (magazine)
   B. Hear My Prayer (compact disc [CD])
   C. Green Acres (television show)
   D. In Praise of Solid People (poem)
   E. The Evening Times (newspaper)

PARTS OF SPEECH:
An infintive phrase is an infinitive plus a word or words.

   Examples: to seem bored
   to watch a play

Circle the infinitive phrase:

3. Ebony and Brian like to read mysteries.

SPELLING:

4. A. Add *er* to swim: _____ D. Add *ly* to lone: _____
   B. Add *ing* to fume: _____ E. Add *en* to damp: _____
   C. Add *y* to ice: _____ F. Add *ed* to cup: _____

SENTENCE COMBINING:

5. Jim and Tessa dined at a small British restaurant.
   The restaurant is noted for serving bubble and squeak.

   _____

   _____

DAY 62

CAPITALIZATION:

1. under the marshall plan, america sent money to europe to help the nations recover from world war II.

PUNCTUATION:

2. Rising to his feet the tall dark haired man asked May I speak for a few minutes

PARTS OF SPEECH: VERBS
 Underline the verb phrase twice:

3. A. You must have (knew, known) her secret.
   B. Have you (swam, swum) in a pond?
   C. Could the baby have (grown, grew) an inch in a month?
   D. She might have (broke, broken) her little finger.
   E. He has (bought, boughten) a fiddle.

TEXT COMPONENTS:

4. A dictionary usually located near the back of a book and used to define terms within that text is a _____.

SENTENCE COMBINING:

5. Jacy is learning to play the guitar.
   It is an electric guitar.
   He practices every afternoon.
   He practices for at least an hour.

   _____

   _____

DAY 63

CAPITALIZATION:

1. did mayor sabo attend a new year's eve party at dr. rand's home for pets without homes foundation?

PUNCTUATION:
Punctuate this friendly letter:

2.
                                      7867 High St
                                      Garrestsville OH   44231
                                      Nov 21 20--

        Dear Candace

                Im thrilled that youre coming to visit us next spring My sisters brothers and cousins will be here also Lets have a family reunion

                                      Sincerely
                                        Alva

PARTS OF SPEECH: ADVERBS/ADJECTIVES
Write the correct word:

3. She startles _____ (easy, easily).

PARTS OF SPEECH: VERBS
Underline the subject once and the verb or verb phrase twice:

4. In the morning, call and confirm our reservations.

SENTENCE COMBINING:

5. Humphrey Bogart starred in the movie entitled *Casa Blanca*. *Casa Blanca* is an American classic.

_____

_____

DAY 64

CAPITALIZATION:
Capitalize this poem by W. H. Auden:

1. in the desert of the heart
   let the healing fountain start,
   in the prison of his days
   teach the free man how to praise.

PUNCTUATION:

2. Lets have a heart to heart talk and well make a decision said their dad

SENTENCES/FRAGMENTS/RUN-ONS:
Write S for sentence, F for fragment, and R-O for run-on:

3. A. ____ A starship is a spacecraft, it's designed for interstellar travel.
   B. ____ Dimming their lights, they slowly approached the accident.
   C. ____ Her grandmother fascinating stories about her youth.

PARTS OF SPEECH: VERBS
Circle the correct verb:
<u>Remember</u>: *To set, to raise,* and *to lay* require a direct object.

4. A. A hot air balloon has (raised, risen) from the desert floor.
   B. Have you been (sitting, setting) here long?
   C. The contractor had (laid, lain) his blueprints on the truck's hood.

SENTENCE COMBINING:

5. The highest temperature recorded for Central Park was 106 degrees.
   This occurred on July 9, 1936.
   Central Park is a famous park in New York City.

   _____

   _____

DAY 65

CAPITALIZATION:

1. andrew mellon, a pittsburgh banker, was secretary of the treasury in the 1920's.

PUNCTUATION:

2. Determined to win the player encouraged his tired troubled teammates

PARTS OF SPEECH: ADJECTIVES
Circle any descriptive adjectives in the following sentence:

3. Traveling through eastern Canada, we saw a small brown tree frog with a shrill, piping call.

PARTS OF SPEECH: CONJUNCTIONS
Write the second word in each pair of correlative conjunctions:

4. A. Both - _____   B. Neither - _____   C. Either - _____

SENTENCE COMBINING:

5. Court bouillon is a liquid.
   It is made with water.
   It is made with vegetables.
   It is made with seasonings.
   It is used to poach fish.

_____

_____

DAY 66

CAPITALIZATION:

1. in the time of moses, palestine was part of the egyptian empire.

PUNCTUATION:

2. Werent you in fact the first in your family to graduate from college Joyce

DICTIONARY SKILLS:

Divide the following words into syllables. Place the accent mark on the syllable that is stressed:

3. A. tremor - _____   C. festival - _____
   B. supply - _____   D. surprisingly - _____

PARTS OF SPEECH: ADJECTIVES

Circle the correct form:

4. A. The firstborn was the (heavier, heaviest) quintuplet.
   B. My mother claims that her sister was (more pampered, most pampered) than she.
   C. Of the three nylon cords, that one is (more elastic, most elastic).

SENTENCE COMBINING:

5. Gregg's grandpa may drive him to his game.
   Gregg's grandma may drive him to his game.
   It is a soccer game.
   It is at four o'clock.

   _____

   _____

DAY 67

CAPITALIZATION:

1. our uncle ed said, "john sevier began nashville as a little village on the cumberland river."

PUNCTUATION:

2. The three senators wives smiled shook hands and then stepped onto the decorated stage

PARTS OF SPEECH:
Circle the correct word:

3. A. Bly and Ander want (there, their, they're) pictures taken.
   B. The taxi cab lost (it's, its) back rear tire.
   C. (Your, You're) suppposed to wait here.
   D. Dr. Ecker will go (to, two, too) the hospital later this evening.

PARTS OF SPEECH: ADJECTIVES
Underline the subject once and the verb twice. Label the predicate adjective-P.A.:

4. Parker's new white kitten is very energetic.

SENTENCE COMBINING:

5. New driving irons have been introduced.
   They hit farther than woods.
   They hit straighter than long irons.

_____

_____

DAY 68

CAPITALIZATION:

1. the nineteenth amendment to the *u. s. constitution* gave women the right to vote.

PUNCTUATION:
Punctuate these types of sentences:

2. A. Hold out your hand (imperative)
   B. I'll help you (declarative)
   C. Has your father seen this (interrogative sentence)
   D. That's right (exclamatory sentence)

PARTS OF SPEECH: NOUNS

Some words ending in o add *s* to form the plural.   ego - egos
Some words ending in o add *es* to form the plural.   tomato - tomatoes
USE A DICTIONARY TO DETERMINE CORRECT SPELLING.
If a dictionary lists two or more possible plurals, the first one is the recommended one.
Example: crescendo n. pl. *dos*, or *does,* also *di*   =   crescendos

Write the plural:

3. A. dynamo - _____   C. tango - _____
   B. motto - _____   D. flamingo - _____

PARTS OF SPEECH: ADVERBS
Circle the correct word:

4. He hardly (never, ever) eats breakfast.

SENTENCE COMBINING:

5. Coconut oil is a fat extracted from coconuts.
   It is used especially in making soaps and food products.

_____

_____

DAY 69

CAPITALIZATION:

1. "did jake plummer, the quarterback for the cardinals, hurt his hand?" asked mrs. carlton.

PUNCTUATION:

2. Thats a cute puppy but hes still too young to take home said Elaine

ANALOGIES:

Complete this analogy:

3. love : cherish :: lenghten : _____
   (a) retract   (b) extend   (c) rekindle   (d) shorten

OBJECTS:

Circle the direct object, box the indirect object, and underline the object of the preposition:

4. At the wedding reception, the bride and groom gave their guests fragrant ivory candles.

SENTENCE COMBINING:

5. A snood was popular in the 1940's.
   A snood is a net or fabric bag pinned at the nape of a woman's neck.
   Its purpose is to hold her hair.

   _____

   _____

DAY 70

CAPITALIZATION:

1. a french sculptor, frederic auguste bartholdi, created the statue of liberty.

PUNCTUATION:

2. At the end of June the Halstead family bought a small French style home out side of Ft Worth

PARTS OF SPEECH: VERBS
Write these contractions:

3. A. here is - _____
   B. I have - _____
   C. you are - _____
   D. I am - _____
   E. he is - _____
   F. we are - _____
   G. they are - _____
   H. had not - _____
   I. what is - _____
   J. has not - _____
   K. we will - _____
   L. would not - _____

PARTS OF SPEECH: PRONOUNS
Circle the antecedent of the boldfaced possessive pronoun:

4. Chasing across the park, the elkhound wagged **its** tail and barked.

SENTENCE COMBINING:

5. The rabbit stopped.
   He nibbled on a blade of grass.
   He hopped on.

   _____

   _____

DAY 71

CAPITALIZATION:

1. abigail adams, wife of president john adams, said, "learning is not attained by chance..."

PUNCTUATION:

2. We cant find Alexanders toy a stuffed giraffe with huge felt eyes

FRIENDLY LETTERS/ENVELOPES:

Write your return address; then, address the envelope to Anthony Bach who receives his mail at Post Office Box 115 in the city of Boulder in the state of Colorado. The zip code is 80328.

3.

PARTS OF SPEECH: ADVERBS

Circle any adverbs that tell *to what extent*:

4. That hostess is not very friendly.

SENTENCE COMBINING:

5. Mr. Kane bought a new watch.
   It can store one hundred phone numbers and email addresses.

DAY 72

CAPITALIZATION:

Capitalize this outline:

1. i. holidays
      a. fourth of july
      b. new year's day
   ii. special days
      a. st. patrick's day
      b. arbor day

PUNCTUATION:

2. Do you Scott have a fifty five gallon drum that I could use   asked Dora

PARTS OF SPEECH: ADJECTIVES

   A proper adjective is derived from a proper noun.
   Example: the city of **Rome**   **Roman**   a **Roman** coin
              the country of **Portugal**   **Portuguese**   **Portuguese** fishermen

3. Santorini is an island of Greece.   Santorini is a _____ island.

PARTS OF SPEECH: VERBS

Write a sentence using the verb *to go* in the past tense; circle the verb:

4. _____

SENTENCE COMBINING:

5. The wedding march began.
   The bride started down the aisle.
   Everyone stood.

   _____

   _____

DAY 73

CAPITALIZATION:

1. the president rose from his desk in the oval office to greet the ambassador from chile.

PUNCTUATION:

2. Although the two girls father doesnt like snow he takes them skiing sledding and ice skating

SENTENCE TYPES:
Write an interrogative sentence:

3. _____

PARTS OF SPEECH: VERBS

Linking verbs do not show action. However, some verbs can serve as an action verb or as a linking verb.

Remember: In deciding if a verb is action or linking, try placing *is, am, are, was,* or *were* in its place. If it doesn't change the sentence meaning, it's usually linking.

Write LV if the verb is linking and AV if the verb is action:

4. A. ____ The baker <u>tasted</u> the filling for the apple pie.
   B. ____ The filling <u>tasted</u> rather sour.

SENTENCE COMBINING:

5. A Kentucky Derby winner was sold.
   The horse was bought by a company from Ireland.
   The horse was sold for approximately $60,000,000.

   _____

   _____

DAY 74

CAPITALIZATION:

1. last year, uncle tito began taking french horn and piano lessons from professor sartor.

PUNCTUATION:

2. Miss Allie Potts has moved her office to 65 E Times Square New York NY 10036

PARTS OF SPEECH: PREPOSITIONS

Circle prepositional phrases; label any object of the preposition-OP:

3. Before the completion of their new home, inspectors checked for faulty wiring.

PARTS OF SPEECH: VERBS

A participle is not a tense. The present participle is formed by adding *ing* to a verb. The past participle is formed by adding <u>ed</u> to regular verbs; irregular verbs change in forming the past participle.

4. A. Write the present participle of *to rehearse*: _____
   B. Write the past participle of *to attract*: __(had)_____
   C. Write the past participle of *to drive*: __(had)_____

SENTENCE COMBINING:

5. Geohydrology studies the character and source of underground water. Caleigh's mother is a geohydrologist.

   _____

   _____

DAY 75

CAPITALIZATION:

1. during an armed forces day parade, captain bailey and his family cheered the local high school band.

PUNCTUATION:

Write the abbreviation for the following:

2. A. avenue - _____   E. Monday - _____
    B. January - _____   F. inch - _____
    C. dozen - _____   G. pint - _____
    D. Thursday - _____   H. centimeter - _____

PARTS OF SPEECH: VERBS

A transitive verb has a direct object; an intransitive verb does not.

Write TV if the verb is transitive; write IV if the verb is intransitive:

3. A. _____ The speaker coughed into the microphone.
    B. _____ She laughed at the silly antics of the seals.
    C. _____ The father rubbed sun protection cream on the toddler's skin.

SUBJECT/VERB:

Underline the compound subject once and the compound verb twice:

4. During weekends, Tricia and her father create and bake different types of cookies.

SENTENCE COMBINING:

5. A White House web site has been redesigned.
   It has more photographs and livelier graphics.
   It is easier to navigate.

_____

_____

DAY 76

CAPITALIZATION:

1. did connie think that the miami heat would win the n.b.a.'s eastern conference championship?

PUNCTUATION:

2. Strong and muscular the contestant lifted a rain filled barrel over his head

DICTIONARY: GUIDE WORDS

Place a √ before a word that will appear on the same dictionary page as the words **egg** and **either**:

3. A. ___ egestion   C. ___ ego   E. ___ eider   G. ___ eight

   B. ___ eidolon   D. ___ eject   F. ___ egret   H. ___ Egyptian

PARTS OF SPEECH: NOUNS

Write the possessive form:

4. A. a bracelet belonging to Angela - _____

   B. several hiking trails belonging to the city - _____

   C. an airplane bought by Mr. and Mrs. Goss - _____
   _____

SENTENCE COMBINING:

5. Beta-carotene is a very important nutrient.
   It is found in carrots.
   It is found in pumpkins.
   It is found in sweet potatoes.
   It is found in red peppers.

   _____
   _____

DAY 77

CAPITALIZATION:

1. they bought mirex* watches at lo wu commercial center in shenzhen, china.
*brand name

PUNCTUATION:

2. In an APA* report   Carlos said   I learned that there are 130 million pets in the U S
*abbreviation for American Pet Association

PARTS OF SPEECH: NOUNS
   Circle any nouns:

3. A hasp is a device usually made of metal and used to fasten doors or lids.

FRIENDLY LETTERS/ENVELOPES:
   The parts of a friendly letter are closing, salutation, heading, body, and signature.

(A) _____
(B) _____,
(C) _____
(D) _____,
(E) _____

   Label the parts of a friendly letter:

4. A. _____   D. _____
    B. _____   E. _____
    C. _____

SENTENCE COMBINING:

5. Joyce works at a bakery after school.
   Joyce's neighbor owns the bakery.

_____

_____

DAY 78

CAPITALIZATION:
Capitalize these titles:

1. A. great quotes from great leaders
    B. "there's an owl in my room"
    C. "the gentleman is cold"

PUNCTUATION:

2. The bridge old and rickety will be restored through a donation by Dr and Mrs Ridd

DICTIONARY: ALPHABETIZING
Place these words in alphabetical order:

    dowel   ditch   drone   daze   downward   dower

3. _____

PHRASES/CLAUSES:
A clause contains a subject and a verb.

A <u>dependent clause</u> does not express a complete thought and cannot stand alone as a sentence. Example: **If I had been with you**

An <u>independent clause</u> expresses a complete thought and can stand alone as a sentence. Example: **Their shower was covered in mildew.**

Write <u>DC</u> if the group of words is a dependent clause; write <u>IC</u> if the group of words is an independent clause:

4. A. _____ Even though he enjoys jazz
    B. _____ A jeweler examined several pearl earrings
    C. _____ Relaxing, he lay on the bed and read

SENTENCE COMBINING:

5. Lindy was the nickname for Charles A. Lindbergh.
   Lindy was also the name of a jitterbug dance.

   _____

   _____

DAY 79

CAPITALIZATION:

1. "did the fox indians live on the great plains?" asked tara.

PUNCTUATION:

2. The show stopping kitchen included granite counters wood cabinets and tile floors Preston

DIFFICULT WORDS:
   Circle the correct word:

3. A. You (can, may) board if you want," said the bus driver.
   B. Marlena exclaimed, "I want to go, (to, two, too)!"
   C. Their friend laughed and said, "I know what (your, you're) thinking."
   D. (There, Their, They're) are no lemons left to make lemonade.
   E. "(It's, Its) wing is hurt," said the bird rescue attendant.

SENTENCES/FRAGMENTS/RUN-ONS:
   Write S for sentence, F for fragment, and R-O for run-on:

4. A. _____ Although she seldom goes to a play.
   B. _____ Licking itself, the cat scanning the room.
   C. _____ Your silence is puzzling, you are never quiet.

SENTENCE COMBINING:

5. Jeremy didn't catch well during the game.
   Jeremy hit a home run during the last inning.

   _____

   _____

DAY 80

CAPITALIZATION:

1. the islam religion which began in arabia in 600 a. d. spread through the middle east.

PUNCTUATION:

2. Gen Robert E Lee surrendered on April 9 1865 at Appomatox Court House

PARTS OF SPEECH: PRONOUNS
Circle the correct pronoun:

3. Kyle, Micah, and (him, he) are going to Cancun next week.

PARTS OF SPEECH: ADJECTIVES

Limiting adjectives do not describe but modify (go over to) a noun or pronoun.
    <u>articles</u> (*a, an,* or *the*):   *a* lion
    <u>numbers</u>:   *four* boxes
    <u>this</u>, <u>that</u>, <u>those</u>, and <u>these</u>:   *this* camera   *these* bricks
                                      that griddle   *those* kilns
    <u>indefinites</u> such as so, many, few, several, no, any: *many* owls

To be adjectives, they must modify *(go over to)* ***a noun or pronoun.***
Circle any limiting adjectives:

4. Thirty trout had been released into that stream a few weeks ago.

SENTENCE COMBINING:

5. A stigil is an instrument.
   It was used by ancient Greeks and Romans.
   It was used to scrape the moisture off skin after bathing.

   _____

   _____

Day 81

CAPITALIZATION:

1. during the 1860's, cattle often were taken on the sedalia trail and then shipped to the east.

PUNCTUATION:

2. Did the Allied invasion of France begin June 6 1944 asked Steven

PARTS OF SPEECH: VERBS
   Underline the subject once and the verb phrase twice:

3. A. He may have already (went, gone) to the campsite.
    B. Did your check (came, come) in the mail?
    C. Dr. Barnett should not have (took, taken) her parents to the lake.
    D. Their horses were (rode, ridden) very slowly at first.

PARTS OF SPEECH: PREPOSITIONS
   Circle any prepositional phrases; label any object of the preposition - **O.P.**:

4. The article about sports cars was located in the last section of the newspaper.

SENTENCE COMBINING:

5. Bovids are animals that have hollow horns in both males and females.
    This family includes antelopes.
    This family includes goats.
    This family includes oxen.

    _____

    _____

DAY 82

CAPITALIZATION:

1. by 1852, the b&o railroad stretched from the atlantic ocean to the mississippi river.

PUNCTUATION:

2. If you want to see The Winters End* it begins at 8 oclock

*name of a television movie

DICTIONARY USAGE:

> **condone** (ken-dōn) v. 1: to forgive or treat as harmless or unimportant
> syn. excuse; condonable (adj.); condoner (n.)

3. A. There are eight parts of speech: noun *(n.)*, **adjective** *(adj.)*, **verb** *(v.)*, **adverb** *(adv.)*, **pronoun** *(pro.)*, **preposition** *(prep.)*, **conjunction** *(conj.)*, and **interjection** *(intj.)*.
   What part of speech is *condone*? _____
   B. What synonym is given for *condone*? _____
   C. I cannot *condone* her actions. What does this sentence mean?
   _____

PARTS OF SPEECH: ADVERBS

Adverbs tell *how*.

Write four adverbs that tell how children may play:

4. _____, _____, _____,
   and _____

SENTENCE COMBINING:

5. The world's oldest working roller coaster is in Altoona, Pennsylvania.
   It was built in 1902.
   It is called Leap the Dips.

   _____

   _____

DAY 83

CAPITALIZATION:

1. does oasis of the desert restaurant serve goat soup and other african foods?

PUNCTUATION:

2. Kali E Coy and her daughter the woman carrying a baby arrived on Worldstar Airlines earlier flight

PARTS OF SPEECH: VERBS

Underline the subject once and the verb or verb phrase twice:

3. A. Has she ever (flew, flown) over Niagara Falls?
    B. The final batter had (come, came) to the plate.
    C. Ice was (froze, frozen) onto the car's door handles.
    D. For the special concert, Jared (sung, sang) a solo.
    E. Her mother may have (threw, thrown) the stale cereal in the garbage.
    F. (Tell, Tells) me your honest opinion.

PARTS OF SPEECH: NOUNS

A predicate nominative occurs after a linking verb and means the same as the subject. A predicate nominative is often a noun.

Underline the subject once and the verb twice; label the predicate nominative-P.N.:

4. Sammy is a guitarist for his church band.

SENTENCE COMBINING:

5. Gary and Heather are making ice cream.
    They are adding crushed ice and rock salt.
    They are adding them to the outside of the cream canister.

_____

_____

DAY 84

CAPITALIZATION:

1. last fall, aunt teresa spoke to our biology class about new zealand's kea bird.

PUNCTUATION:

2. Youre expected Martha to stay for a long leisurely lunch   said Ms Elton

PARTS OF SPEECH: ADJECTIVES/PRONOUNS

This, that, those, and *these* may serve as adjectives or pronouns.

Examples: **This** slate feels rough.   This what?   slate   **adjective**
This feels rough.   (You don't know what feels rough.)   **pronoun**

Write **ADJ.** if the boldfaced word serves as an adjective and **PRO.** if the boldfaced word serves as a pronoun:

3. A. _____   **That** parachute was defective.

   B. _____   **This** is an interesting situation.

   C. _____   Would you like **these** bottles sterilized?

PARTS OF SPEECH: NOUNS

Write the possessive form:

4. A. matted hair on a dog - _____

   B. a party given by two girls - _____

   C. a game played by many children - _____

SENTENCE COMBINING:

5. The Clark Company began in 1886.
   It was located in Pittsburgh, Pennsylvania.
   It made candy bars.

   _____

   _____

DAY 85

CAPITALIZATION:

1. "i think," said mrs. lu, "that you'd like to visit oxcart museum in costa rica."

PUNCTUATION:
Punctuate these titles:

2. A. The Use of Metaphors   (essay)
   B. Investments   (magazine)
   C. Jack and Jill   (nursery rhyme)
   D. Power of Your Love   (song)

SENTENCE TYPES:
Write an exclamatory sentence:

3. _____

PREFIXES/ROOTS/SUFFIXES:
Prefixes have meaning and help to understand the meaning of a word.

uni, mono = 1	*anti* = against	*ir, im, il, un, non* = not
bi, du = 2	*super* = highest	*de, dis* = away from
tri = 3	*post* = after	*re* = again or backwards
quad = 4	*trans* = across	*fore, pre, ante* = before

Divide each word into prefix + root; explain its meaning:

4. A. monosyllable - _____ _____
   B. postdate - _____ _____
   C. recline - _____ _____
   D. distract - _____ _____

SENTENCE COMBINING:

5. A deerstalker is a type of hat.
   It has earflaps.
   It has a visor in the front and in the back.

   _____

   _____

DAY 86

CAPITALIZATION:

1. the house of commons is part of england's governing body called parliament.

PUNCTUATION:

Punctuate this friendly letter:

2.
                                                    12 Broad Blvd
                                                    St Louis MO 99999
                                                    Feb 12 20--

    Dear Siggy

        My cousins their friends and my Aunt Mabel from Memphis Tennessee will be visiting next week   Why dont you visit us too

                                                      Your friend
                                                      Walt

PARTS OF SPEECH: VERBS

Circle any infinitive phrases:

3. Jemima wants to become a park ranger.

LIBRARY SKILLS:

4. A/An _____ is a book containing maps.

SENTENCE COMBINING:

5. Gail buys a special hair conditioner.
   It adds strength and elasticity to her hair.
   Her hair is damaged.

_____

_____

DAY 87

CAPITALIZATION:
Capitalize this poem:

1. lives of great men remind us
   we can make our lives sublime,
   and, departing, leave behind us
   footprints on the sands of time.
       -henry wadsworth longfellow

PUNCTUATION:

2. When Sen Smiths son arrived at 4 30 he was met by his mother in laws sister

PARTS OF SPEECH: PREPOSITIONS
Underline the subject once and the verb twice. Circle any prepositional phrase; label any object of the preposition-O.P.:

3. Last evening, Chan went with his aunt and uncle to a baseball game.

SPELLING:
When do you use *er* and *or* endings? If you aren't certain, use a dictionary. However, there is a rule that works frequently.
 If *tion* or *ion* can be added to a root word, that word *usually* adds *or* as the *suffix*.

 Examples: deliberate delibera**tion** deliberat**or**
      educate   educa**tion**   educat**or**

	word	*tion* form	*ir* form
4. A.	create	_____	_____
B.	designate	_____	_____

SENTENCE COMBINING:

5. Kama gets headaches occasionally.
   She then drinks herbal tea and takes a nap.

_____

_____

DAY 88

CAPITALIZATION:

1. as a gift for st. valentine's day, beverly bought a gorgo* watch for her grandmother.
*brand name

PUNCTUATION:

2. Cool Ive found a Civil War sword   exclaimed Eric

PARTS OF SPEECH: NOUNS
Some words ending in **f** add **s** to form the plural.
  Example: puff - puffs
Some words ending in **f** change **f** to **v** and add **es** to form the plural.
  Example: leaf - leaves

USE A DICTIONARY TO DETERMINE CORRECT SPELLING.
Write the plural:

3. A. half - _____ C. cuff - _____

 B. loaf - _____ D. send-off - _____

COMPOUND/COMPLEX/COMPOUND-COMPLEX SENTENCES:
A compound sentence contains two or more complete thoughts and is usually joined by a conjunction.
  Example: *His mother is a judge,* <u>and</u> *his father has a home-based business.*
       Your idea is very creative, <u>but</u> *it needs more thought..*

Place a √ before a compound sentence:

4. A. _____ His opinion is highly valued by the entire staff.
 B. _____ Joy joined the Navy in 1960 and later became a civil service worker.
 C. _____ Kerry has a keen interest in songwriting, and she wants to attend a college in Nashville.

SENTENCE COMBINING:

5. The cinnamon buns are hot and have a tempting aroma.
 They were just taken from the oven.

_____

_____

DAY 89

CAPITALIZATION:
Capitalize this outline:

1.   i. canadian eastern provinces
       a. quebec
       b. new brunswick
  ii. canadian western provinces
       a. alberta
       b. yukon

PUNCTUATION:

2. His speech most certainly reflects his strong positive position on that issue

PARTS OF SPEECH: CONJUNCTIONS
Write two sentences containing correlative conjunctions:

3. A. _____

    B. _____

PARTS OF SPEECH: INTERJECTIONS
Circle any interjections:

4. Jordan screamed, "Far out! I've been accepted by Yale!"

SENTENCE COMBINING:

5. She visited the Smithsonian's National Museum of American History website.
She saw the earliest hand-written manuscript of a famous poem.
The poem was Francis Scott Key's "Star Spangled Banner."

_____

_____

DAY 90

CAPITALIZATION:

1. "in roman mythology, janus was an important god," explained the tour guide.

PUNCTUATION:

Punctuate this inside address and salutation of a business letter:

2. Baby Carriage Express
   P O Box 1
   Hyattsville MD   20781

   Dear Mrs Payne

TEXT COMPONENTS:

3. A special dictionary of geographical terms often found in the back of geography and history texts is: (a) index   (b) gazeteer   (c) atlas   (d) bibliography

PARTS OF SPEECH: NOUNS

Write a propr noun for each common noun:

4. A. canal - _____
    B. university - _____
    C. battle - _____

SENTENCE COMBINING:

5. Marco is preoccupied writing a novel.
   Marco sometimes skips meals.
   The novel is a mystery novel.

   _____
   _____

DAY 91

CAPITALIZATION:

1. under president wilson, congress set up the federal trade commission to regulate businesses.

PUNCTUATION:

2. Please write to the following address   Dr Susan Rath 404 S Middle Street Grand Rapids MI   49501

ANALOGIES:
Complete this analogy:

3. humble : arrogant :: hibernate : _____
   (a) reticent   (b) bear   (c) dormant   (d) activate

PARTS OF SPEECH: ADJECTIVES/ADVERBS
Write the correct word:

4. Stop acting so _____ (weirdly, weird).

SENTENCE COMBINING:

5. The coach had been offered a prominent college job.
   The job was coaching basketball.
   The job was in his home state.
   He turned down the offer.

   _____

   _____

DAY 92

CAPITALIZATION:

1. they traveled through yakima valley and over stampede pass of the cascade mountains.

PUNCTUATION:

2. Can you Mrs Devon send two letters three post cards and an email to me

PARTS OF SPEECH: ADVERBS
   Circle any adverbs:

3. We don't often go downtown to shop.

DIFFICULT WORDS:
   Circle the correct word:

4. A. (There, Their, They're) isn't any milk for my cereal.
   B. The mechanic's estimate was (to, two, too) high.
   C. His job had been (affected, effected) by his negative attitude.
   D. (May, Can) you unlock this deadbolt?

SENTENCE COMBINING:

5. Mrs. Coyle decided to open her business in a mall.
   Mrs. Coyle has a hardware store.
   Mrs. Coyle signed a long-term lease.

   _____

   _____

DAY 93

CAPITALIZATION:

1. we took capitol beltway to kenilworth avenue to find a mexican food cafe.

PUNCTUATION:

2. Stomping his feet Joe brushed the caked icy snow from his brown leather boots

ANTONYMS/SYNONYMS/HOMONYMS:

Antonyms are words with opposite meanings.
Synonyms are words with similar meanings.
Homonyms are words that are spelled differently but sound alike.

3. A. An antonym for foolish is _____.
   B. A synonym for gruesome is _____.
   C. A homonym for gate is _____.

PARTS OF SPEECH: VERBS

Circle the correct verb:

Remember: *To set, to raise,* and *to lay* require a direct object.

4. A. The patient was (lying, laying) on her side to read.
   B. He (sat, set) quietly while the photographer adjusted the camera.
   C. Their sister (raises, rises) sheep on a Montana ranch.

SENTENCE COMBINING:

5. Kit signed for the delivered package.
   Kit shook the package.
   Kit handed it to his father.

   _____

   _____

DAY 94

CAPITALIZATION:

1. did dad read the magazine, <u>western ways</u>, during his armed forces day weekend trip?

PUNCTUATION:

2. Jules Leotard the inventor of the leotard performed in Paris France in 1859

PARTS OF SPEECH: NOUNS

An appositive is a word or group of words that stands next to a noun and adds additional information.

    Example: My friend, **Dakota**, is funny.
                   Dakota, **the young man in the blue shirt**, is funny.

Rewrite this sentence using an appositive:

3. Mr. Hart is Jan's father. Mr. Hart is a foreman for a large construction company.

_____

DICTIONARY SKILLS:

Place the accent mark on the stressed syllable. Write a short definition for each word:

4. A. mi nute - _____

   B. min ute - _____

SENTENCE COMBINING:

5. Stan shopped for furnishings for his townhouse.
Stan purchased a brown leather sofa.
Stan purchased a Navajo rug.

_____

_____

DAY 95

CAPITALIZATION:

1. is haast pass near clutha river in the northeastern section of queensland, new zealand?

PUNCTUATION:

2. Having taken a bus we werent able to stop at Ciscos house on River Rd

PARTS OF SPEECH: ADVERBS
   Circle the correct form:

3. A.   She raised the sail (more vigorously, most vigorously) on her third try.
   B.   Jackie speaks French (more fluently, most fluently) than her sister.
   C.   During the fifth competition, he swam (faster, fastest).

PARTS OF SPEECH: ADJECTIVES
   A proper adjective is derived from a proper noun.
   Example: the continent of **Asia**   **Asian**   an **Asian** beetle

   Sometimes, a proper adjective is the same as the proper noun form.
   Example: the state of **Indiana**   **Indiana**   an **Indiana** farm

   Write the proper adjective form of the boldfaced proper noun:

4. A.   the **Infaco Company**: _____ baby food
   B.   a country in **Latin America**: a _____ country

SENTENCE COMBINING:

5. In 1914, Robert Goddard proposed that man could travel to the moon.
   He was ridiculed by newspapers.
   He was called the "moon man."

   _____

   _____

DAY 96

CAPITALIZATION:

1. yesterday, i purchased a clarbon* bracelet, a christmas gift for grandmother.
*brand name

PUNCTUATION:

2. William James the writer said The deepest principle in human nature is the craving to be appreciated

DICTIONARY: ALPHABETIZING
   Place these words in alphabetical order:
   crypt   croissant   creed   crinoline   creme   crime
3. _____

FRIENDLY LETTERS/ENVELOPES:
   Write your return address:
4. _____
   _____
   _____
   _____
                    _____
                    _____
                    _____
   _____

SENTENCE COMBINING:

5. My dad and uncle have great senses of humor.
   My dad likes to play jokes on my uncle.
   My uncle likes to play jokes on my dad.

   _____
   _____

DAY 97

CAPITALIZATION:

1. their new pets, a siamese cat and a basset hound, had been given to the appleton twins as easter presents.

PUNCTUATION:

2. Because the childs crying hadnt stopped his mother soothed him rocked him and read him a story

PARTS OF SPEECH: ADJECTIVES
Circle any descriptive adjectives.   Label the predicate adjective-P.A.:

3. A polonaise, a dress with a fitted waist and a draped cutaway overskirt, is usually elaborate.

PARTS OF SPEECH: ADVERBS
Circle the correct word:

4. A. Mandy doesn't have (nothing, anything) to drink.
   B. "Stop acting so (stupid, stupidly)," his friend said.
   C. That family scarcely has (any, no) time to visit friends and relatives.

SENTENCE COMBINING:

5. Gateau was served at a luncheon.
   Gateau was the dessert.
   Gateau is a rich cake.
   Gateau is a fancy cake.

_____

_____

DAY 98

CAPITALIZATION:

1. lennox lewis, a british athlete, boxed at the thomas mack center at the university of las vegas.

PUNCTUATION:

2. Her parents boarded the Pandy a restaurant ship that left Alexandria Virginia

PHRASES AND CLAUSES:
  Circle the dependent clause:

3. When the dog went to training classes, he was fed treats for positive reinforcement.

PARTS OF SPEECH: PRONOUNS
  Circle the correct pronoun:

4. The announcer, the producer, and (they, them) laughed about the child's remark.

SENTENCE COMBINING:

5. Tickets are available for Hong Kong.
   Tickets are available for Singapore.
   Tickets are available for Bangkok.
   They are airline tickets.
   They are discounted.

   _____

   _____

DAY 99

CAPITALIZATION:

1. can you take a double-decker bus from trafalgar square the entire way to bath, once a roman city?

PUNCTUATION:

2. From Oct 1 until Thanksgiving St Claire Blvd will be closed from 4 to 9 P M

COMPOUND/COMPLEX/COMPOUND-COMPLEX SENTENCES:
A compound sentence contains two or more complete thoughts and is usually joined by a conjunction.

Place a √ before a compound sentence:

3. A. _____ Our computer was delivered today, but it was broken in transit.
   B. _____ Ricardo patted the horse's head and offered a carrot.

PARTS OF SPEECH: NOUNS
A gerund is a noun that is formed by adding *ing* to a verb.

Example: **Swimming** is fun. (*Swimming* is a noun serving as the subject.)

A gerund phrase = gerund + words

Example: **Swimming in a lake** is fun.

Change each gerund to a gerund phrase:

4. A. They enjoy watching_____.
   B. Standing _____ can be boring.

SENTENCE COMBINING:

5. The three teenagers had their picture taken.
   They gave it to their mother as a Christmas present.
   Their mother cried.

   _____

   _____

DAY 100

CAPITALIZATION:

1. "have you eaten irish soda bread with jam?" asked tom. "it's delicious!"

PUNCTUATION:

2. Franco said By the way Gina youre my sisters favorite drama instructor

PARTS OF SPEECH: VERBS

3. A. Write the past participle of *to detain*: __(had)_____
   B. Write the present participle of *to encourage*: _____
   C. Write the past participle of *to bring*: __(had)_____

SENTENCES/FRAGMENTS/RUN-ONS:
Write <u>S</u> for sentence, <u>F</u> for fragment, and <u>R-O</u> for run-on:

4. A. ____ Cheerful and alert, the motorist to the construction workers.
   B. ____ An adult stork makes hissing sounds.
   C. ____ A siren wailed volunteer firemen rushed to their autos.
   D. ____ Stop.

SENTENCE COMBINING:

5. My grandmother is German.
   She makes an excellent coffee cake.
   She places streusel topping on it.

   _____

   _____

DAY 101

CAPITALIZATION:

1. he is a nurse at laurel community hospital located on van winkle street in laurel, idaho.

PUNCTUATION:
Place a dash (the width of M) or parentheses ( ) to provide additional information.
Example: My son (the one you met) won a trip to Spain.
Place brackets [ ] to include information within parentheses.
Example: My son (the one you met [the wrestler]) won a trip to Spain.

2. Soft and cuddly the puppy whimpered not because he was hurt

DICTIONARY: GUIDE WORDS

Place a √ before a word that will appear on the same dictionary page as the words **low** and **lunar**:

3. A. ___ low-level   C. ___ lurid   E. ___ love   G. ___ lunacy

   B. ___ luscious   D. ___ loyal   F. ___ lune   H. ___ lounge

PARTS OF SPEECH: VERBS
The perfect tense is formed by adding a form of *to have* to a past participle.
  Present Perfect = *has* or *have* + past participle   (have gone or has gone)
  Past Perfect = *had* + past participle   (had gone)
  Future Perfect = *shall have* or *will have* + past participle
      (will have gone or shall have gone)

Write the tense of the underlined verb phrase:

4. _____   "I <u>have written</u> a check," said Mira.

SENTENCE COMBINING:

5. That new computer is the size of two basketball courts.
   It weighs 106 tons.
   It is able to perform 12.3 trillion operations per second.

_____

_____

DAY 102

CAPITALIZATION:

1. did you watch marso's* annual parade on the vision** channel last thanksgiving?

*department store
**studio name

PUNCTUATION:

2. Whenever Jodys cousin visits from Florida she brings sun ripened oranges and tangerines   remarked Mrs Quade

DICTIONARY USAGE:

> **murky** (mer-kē) adj. 1: dimness caused by smoke, fog, or smog 2: characterized by thickness of air 3: darkly vague or obscure
> murkily (adv.); murkiness (n.)

3. A. There are eight parts of speech: noun *(n.)*, adjective *(adj.)*, verb *(v.)*, adverb *(adv.)*, pronoun *(pro.)*, preposition *(prep.)*, conjunction *(conj.)*, and interjection *(intj.)*.

   What is the adverb form of *murky*? _____

   B. How many syllables make up the noun form? _____

   C. Because your reasoning is *murky*, I cannot understand your point of view. Which definition best fits the use of *murky* in the above sentence? _____

SENTENCE TYPES:

Write an imperative sentence:

4. _____

SENTENCE COMBINING:

5. That man is a highly regarded surrealist artist.
   An exhibit of his works was established at the Radisto Art Museum.

   _____

   _____

DAY 103

CAPITALIZATION:
Capitalize these titles:

1. A. "coat of many colors"
   B. winnie-the-pooh christmas tail
   C. i was born a slave

PUNCTUATION:

2. A childrens theater presented The Grinch a musical based on a story by Dr Seuss

PHRASES/CLAUSES:
A clause contains a subject and a verb.

> A <u>dependent clause</u> does not express a complete thought and, therefore, cannot stand alone as a sentence.
> Example: Whenever a fly lands

> An <u>independent clause</u> expresses a complete thought and is a sentence.
> Example: Smiling, she accepted the award.

Write <u>DC</u> if the group of words is a dependent clause; write <u>IC</u> if the group of words is an independent clause:

3. A. _____ The swimmer gasped for air
   B. _____ Although we're taking the next flight
   C. _____ A shrill noise resounded through the hall

PARTS OF SPEECH: PREPOSITIONS
List fifteen prepositions:

4. _____

SENTENCE COMBINING:

5. Martin has never been to Delaware.
   His cousin lives near Lewes Beach, and he wants to visit.

_____

_____

DAY 104

CAPITALIZATION:

1. "you can visit kartchner caverns located southeast of tucson," said miss thai.

PUNCTUATION:

2. In Whos Who Among Americas Teachers* her name appeared as Samuels G L

*title of a book

PARTS OF SPEECH: PRONOUNS

Objective pronouns are <u>me</u>, <u>him</u>, <u>her</u>, <u>us</u>, <u>them</u>, <u>whom</u>, <u>you</u>, and <u>it</u>.
Objective pronouns serve as objects: direct object
                                         indirect object
                                         object of the preposition

Write <u>D.O.</u> for direct object, <u>I.O.</u> for indirect object, and <u>O.P.</u> for object of the preposition:

3. A. _____ She read *Bambi* to her children and **me**.

   B. _____ He shocked **us** with his tale of being robbed.

   C. _____ The pastor served **them** communion.

SENTENCES/FRAGMENTS/RUN-ONS:

Change this fragment to a sentence:

4. After a brief discussion, decided to buy two new tires.

_____

SENTENCE COMBINING:

5. Jaguars are larger than leopards.
   Jaguars are stockier than leopards.
   Jaguars live chiefly in Central America and South America.

_____

_____

DAY 105

CAPITALIZATION:

1. mandy and i stayed at the relondo resort hotel in ohio for a convention of the a.i.s.* last november.

*abbreviation for Association of International Schools

PUNCTUATION:

2. On Feb 15 1898 the U S S Maine* exploded in Havana Cuba
*name of a ship

SENTENCES/FRAGMENTS/RUN-ONS:
Change this run-on sentence to an acceptable sentence:

3. A marabou is a type of stork, it has a pouch of pink skin at its neck.

_____

PARTS OF SPEECH: VERBS
Write TV if the verb is transitive; write IV if the verb is intransitive:

4. A. _____ No trespassing signs have been posted on the property.
   B. _____ The salesperson asked the client her opinion.
   C. _____ Amerigo Vespucci visited islands off South America in 1497.

SENTENCE COMBINING:

5. One thousand American women were polled.
   They were asked about their skin-care routine.
   Sixty-two percent polled said they spend five minutes or less on their routine.

_____

_____

DAY 106

CAPITALIZATION:

1. while hiking the trails of bandelier national monument, i used bastec* herbal gel to soothe my dry lips.

*brand name

PUNCTUATION:

2. My mothers favorite painting by Thomas Kinkade is entitled Deer Creek Cottage

PARTS OF SPEECH: VERBS

Circle the correct form:

3. A. She has (beat, beaten) me at ping pong.
   B. The tie had been (broke, broken) during the second round.
   C. Our dog could have (drunk, drank) my milkshake.
   D. Mr. Jacobs might have (went, gone) to early church.
   E. Her mother hadn't (ran, run) any errands during the afternoon.

PARTS OF SPEECH: PRONOUNS

4. Dev and Jenny played Kimi and (him, he) in a game of darts.

SENTENCE COMBINING:

5. The Clydesdale horse is a heavy horse.
   It is a draft horse.
   It has feathering on the legs.
   It originated in Clydesdale, Scotland.

_____

_____

DAY 107

CAPITALIZATION:

1. the phoenix suns departed on a trans cantos airlines jet bound for seattle.

PUNCTUATION:

2. The hotel off Rte 1 has thirty three rooms and a well mannered professional staff

PARTS OF SPEECH:
Our language is easier if the relationship between words is understood.

   Example: perjury - noun: a voluntary violation of an oath by false swearing
   perjure - verb: to swear falsely under oath
   perjurious - adjective: marked by false testimony

Write *perjury*, *perjure*, or *perjurious* to complete the sentence:

3. His _____ testimony shocked everyone.

PARTS OF SPEECH: NOUNS
   Circle any nouns:

4. For a project, two children made a tepee covered with skins like those used by the Indians of the Plains.

SENTENCE COMBINING:

5. The house was built in 1931 in Beverly Hills.
   It was built by George R. Kress.
   Kress was in the house-moving business.

   _____

   _____

DAY 108

CAPITALIZATION:

1. "did i mention," asked tanner, "that councilwoman willis bought a regal* minivan?"
   *brand name

PUNCTUATION:

2. This ski package entitles you to a one day lift ticket for any of the following Mt Risa Ski Area Alpine Mountain Ski Area or Shanita

PARTS OF SPEECH: NOUNS
Underline the subject once and the verb twice; label the predicate nominative-P.N.:

4. Their father became a pilot for Air America.

PREFIXES/ROOTS/SUFFIXES:
Prefixes have meaning and help to understand the meaning of a word.

uni, mono = 1	*ab* = not, away from	*ir, im, il, un, non* = not
bi, du = 2	*anti* = against	*super* = highest
tri = 3	*trans* = across	*fore, pre, ante* = before

Divide each word into prefix + root; explain its meaning:

4. A. abnormal - _____ _____
   B. bilingual - _____ _____

SENTENCE COMBINING:

5. Boxing Day is a legal holiday in England.
   It has nothing to do with the sport of boxing.

   _____

   _____

DAY 109

CAPITALIZATION:

1. did capt. w. clark of the lewis and clark expedition explore native american lands?

PUNCTUATION:

2. No we didnt find your shoe however weve located the missing key under your bed

PARTS OF SPEECH:

Write *their, there,* or *they're:*

3. _____ joining _____ friends for an ice cream social.

PARTS OF SPEECH: ADJECTIVES

Limiting adjectives do not describe but modify (go over to) a noun or pronoun.

    articles (*a, an,* or *the*):   *the* taxes
    numbers: *thirty* voters
    this, that, those, and these: *this* pressure   *these* contracts
                                     that wiring   *those* refusals
    indefinites such as so, many, few, several, no, any: *several* disturbances

To be adjectives, they must modify (go over to) **a noun or pronoun.**

Circle any limiting adjectives:

4. The last owner planted several bushes and thirteen trees along these low walls.

SENTENCE COMBINING:

5. Clay may take prizes to the reunion.
Clay's sister may take prizes to the reunion.
The prizes are for the softball tournament winners.

_____

_____

DAY 110

CAPITALIZATION:

1. for thanksgiving dinner, i served oregon salmon, a greek salad, and new york cheese cake.

PUNCTUATION:

2. Rising early Mr Daniels worked on several architects proposals for a beach house

ANALOGIES:
Complete this analogy:

3. hands : clock :: needle : _____
   (a) thread   (b) compass   (c) force   (d) silver

PARTS OF SPEECH: PRONOUNS
Circle the antecedent of the boldfaced word:

4. At the beach, several girls laid **their** blankets side by side.

SENTENCE COMBINING:

5. Wampum was beads of polished shells.
   It was strung in strands, belts, or sashes.
   It was used by Native Americans.
   It was used as money, as ceremonial pledges, and as ornaments.

   _____

   _____

DAY 111

CAPITALIZATION:

1. many people living in the new england states were displeased with the decision that began the war of 1812.

PUNCTUATION:
Write the abbreviation for the following:

2. A. September - _____   E. Northeast - _____

   B. President - _____   F. February - _____

   C. mile - _____   G. Friday - _____

   D. Wednesday - _____   H. meter - _____

PARTS OF SPEECH: ADJECTIVES
Circle the correct adjective form:

3. Of the two pictures, I think this one is (more suitable, most suitable) for framing.

PARTS OF SPEECH: ADJECTIVES/ADVERBS
Write the correct word:

4. The baby had been born _____ (premature, prematurely).

SENTENCE COMBINING:

5. An umiak is an open boat.
   It is made of a wooden frame.
   It is covered with hide.
   It is an Eskimo boat.

   _____

   _____

DAY 112

CAPITALIZATION:

1. born in moscow, russia, peter the great was the only son of czar alexis.

PUNCTUATION:
   Punctuate this friendly letter:

2.   Rte 9
   (A)   Hadley NY   12820
                 Dec 12 20--

   (B)   Dear Chrissy
              Life hasnt been the same since you moved
   (C)   to Salem By the way some of my friends think you
              live in Salem Massachusetts rather than in Oregon
                                    (D)   Your very best pal
                                    (E)   Liz

DICTIONARY: ALPHABETIZING
   Place these words in alphabetical order:

   heifer   heel   helmet   heir   height   helm

3. _____

FRIENDLY LETTERS/ENVELOPES:
   Use the letter in #2 to label the friendly letter parts:

4.   A. _____   D. _____
     B. _____   E. _____
     C. _____

SENTENCE COMBINING:

5. Email has become popular.
   Specialty card shops are declining.

   _____

   _____

DAY 113

CAPITALIZATION:

1. "did rev. rios," asked trent, "buy a prontigo* convertible at lulo motors in the west?"

*brand name

PUNCTUATION:

2. His decision I believe was to order the following for floats twenty one qts of ice cream eight cases of root beer and straws

PARTS OF SPEECH: NOUNS
   Some words change to a new word or add an unusual ending to form the plural.   child - children   octopus - octopi
            father-in-law - fathers-in-law   writ of assistance - writs of assistance
   Some words do not change to form the plural.
            sheep - sheep

   Write the plural:

3. A. shrimp - _____   C. daughter-in-law - _____
   B. ox - _____   D. partner in crime - _____

COMPOUND/COMPLEX/COMPOUND-COMPLEX SENTENCES:
   A complex sentence contains one independent (main) clause and one or more dependent (subordinate) clauses.
      Example: When Tammy has a headache, she lies down for a few hours.
                    dependent clause   *independent clause*
   Place a √ before a complex sentence:
4. A. _____   If it drizzles all morning, the construction crew goes home.
   B. _____   They raced to the barn and climbed up to the hayloft.

SENTENCE COMBINING:

5. Jolene and Paco built storage cabinets in their garage.
   They were tired of the clutter.
   They installed bike braces for their mountain bikes.

   _____

   _____

DAY 114

CAPITALIZATION:

1. "do you," asked professor kent, "know when the bronze age occurred?"

PUNCTUATION:

2. Well Im not sure but Ill be happy to ask my brother in law about it

PARTS OF SPEECH: CONJUNCTIONS

Select the correct verb in this sentence containing correlative conjunctions. Then, circle the correlative conjunctions:

3. Neither Mia nor her brothers (like, likes) to get up early.

PARTS OF SPEECH: NOUNS

Write the possessive form:

4. A. a guitar belonging to Cass - _____

   B. boxes provided by a moving company - _____

   C. a hive shared by more than one bee - _____

SENTENCE COMBINING:

5. Chairs and lamps lay on their sides.
   Files were scattered everywhere.
   The room had been ransacked.

   _____

   _____

DAY 115

CAPITALIZATION:

1. though born during the great depression, he became a director for cladesti investment corporation in the east.

PUNCTUATION:
Punctuate this inside address and salutation of a business letter:

2. Yassie Computer Consulting
   4555 E Stoll Ave
   Rockland ME   04841

   Dear Sir

LIBRARY SKILLS:

3. A. A dictionary that provides information about places is a _____ dictionary.
   B. _____ books have invented stories.
   C. The three types of cards in a card catalog are _____, _____, and _____.

PARTS OF SPEECH: ADVERBS
Circle the correct adverb form:

4. This twin speaks (more distinctly, distincter) than her sister.

SENTENCE COMBINING:

5. The girl had her hair styled for the banquet.
   Before that, she had a manicure.
   The hair style was a bouffant.

   _____

   _____

DAY 116

CAPITALIZATION:

1. because grandfather has diabetes, he has been given a special diet by a nutritionist at colonial nursing home.

PUNCTUATION:

2. The shuttle service isnt on time therefore well call a taxi Sharon

PARTS OF SPEECH:

Write a sentence that includes an infinitive phrase:

3. _____

BUSINESS LETTERS/ENVELOPES:

There are many variations to a business letter. Use this model in labeling the parts. A business letter also includes an inside address and a printed signature as well as a written signature.

4. A. _____ E. _____
    B. _____ F. _____
    C. _____ G. _____
    D. _____

SENTENCE COMBINING:

5. Danny and Arrow found a wallet in a store.
   It was lying on the floor.
   They took it to the lost and found department.

DAY 117

CAPITALIZATION:

1. they want to visit suva lighthouse in the fiji islands of the pacific ocean.

PUNCTUATION:

2. At the beginning of your third sentence you havent added ed to the verb Vicki

PARTS OF SPEECH: NOUNS

Write a proper noun for each common noun:

3. A. trail - _____

   B. county - _____

   C. explorer - _____

SPELLING:

Many words have the <u>ie</u> spelling for long *e* or long *i*:   field   pie
The long *e* sound after <u>c</u> is sometimes spelled <u>ei</u>:   receive
The <u>ei</u> and <u>eigh</u> spelling can say long *a:*   veil   weigh
USE A DICTIONARY WHEN NECESSARY.

Circle the correct spelling:

4. A. relief   releif   D. preist   priest
   B. deceive   decieve   E. percieve   perceive
   C. sliegh   sleigh   F. lien   lein

SENTENCE COMBINING:

5. A magic square is a square with numbers.
   The numbers are arranged so that their sum is the same in each row.
   The numbers are arranged so that their sum is the same in each column.
   The numbers are arranged so that their sum is the same in the main diagonals.

   _____

   _____

DAY 118

CAPITALIZATION:

1. the english essayist, thomas carlyle, said, "the true university of these days is a collection of books."

PUNCTUATION:

2. Theyre adding three fourths cup of small diced marshmallows to the bread batter but it shouldnt affect its taste

SENTENCE TYPES:

Place correct end punctuation and label each sentence type:

3. A. _____ Wow! We did it
   B. _____ A prairie dog is in the squirrel family
   C. _____ Take my hand, please
   D. _____ Do you like pickle relish

PARTS OF SPEECH: PRONOUNS

A relative clause can begin with *who*, *that*, or *which*.
Remember: A clause contains a subject and a verb. A dependent clause cannot stand alone as a complete thought.

Example: The woman **who** just **caught** the football is my aunt.

Circle any relative clause:

4. My grandfather who lives in Boston makes delicious ginger cookies.

SENTENCE COMBINING:

5. Nearly ten million dollars in renovations had been completed. Then, Washington Monument reopened.

_____

_____

DAY 119

CAPITALIZATION:

1. the movie, <u>the magic of flight,</u> was being shown at the theater of the henry ford museum in dearborn, michigan.

PUNCTUATION:

2. I found numerous travel agents ads in the Evening Tribune* said Kirk

*name of a newspaper

TEXT COMPONENTS:

```
INTERJECTIONS.............................................................301
CONJUNCTIONS............................................................305
ADJECTIVES..................................................................309
   Limiting Adjectives    309
      Function    316
      Descriptive Adjectives    319
```

Use the excerpt from this table of contents to answer these questions:

3. A. To which page will you turn to find a chapter entitled "Conjunctions"? _____
   B. Information concerning limiting adjectives can be found between pages _____ and _____.

PARTS OF SPEECH: PRONOUNS
Circle the correct reflexive pronoun:

4. The doorman wants to greet the owner (himself, hisself).

SENTENCE COMBINING:

5. Sir Winston Churchhill was a war correspondent during the Boer War.
   He was captured.
   He escaped.

_____

_____

DAY 120

CAPITALIZATION:

1. students at blake middle school participated in a european cultural fair in may.

PUNCTUATION:
Punctuate these titles:

2. A. Don't Miss Out   (book)
   B. The Basic Brandenburg Concertos   (compact disk [CD])
   C. Man's Best Friend   (short story)
   D. Daily Times   (newspaper)
   E. Healthy Treats Your Pets Will Love   (magazine article)

PARTS OF SPEECH: VERBS

3. The present participle form of *to run* is _____.

PARTS OF SPEECH: VERBS/INTERJECTIONS
Underline the subject once and the verb or verb phrase twice; circle any interjections:

4. Oh! No! One of our teammates has forgotten his airline ticket!

SENTENCE COMBINING:

5. Kuchen is a German food.
   Kuchen is a custard-like coffee cake.
   Kuchen is the official state dessert for South Dakota.

   _____

   _____

DAY 121

CAPITALIZATION:

1. "was this photograph, grandmother," darla asked, "taken at a montana motel last labor day weekend?"

PUNCTUATION:

2. Marla explained Dwight D Eisenhowers farm my friends was in Gettysburg Pennsylvania my hometown

PARTS OF SPEECH: NOUNS

An appostive is a word or group of words that stands next to a noun and adds additional information.

   Examples: Lana Colby, **sister of the bride**, was maid of honor.
              Peppy, **their beagle**, jumps on everyone.

Circle any appositives:

3. Whenever Looty, his Siamese kitten, feels frisky, he jumps on Meg, his little niece.

COMPOUND/COMPLEX/COMPOUND-COMPLEX SENTENCES:

A complex sentence contains one independent (main) clause and one or more dependent (subordinate) clauses.

   Example: After they washed their car, they dried it with a special cloth.
              dependent clause   *independent clause*

Place a √ before a complex sentence:

4. A. _____ Logan won't be attending the fair because he's leaving for Buffalo.
   B. _____ After a trek to the creek, the children sat under a tree and talked.
   C. _____ After I finish eating supper, I have to load the dishwasher.

SENTENCE COMBINING:

5. The girl was pale and frightened.
   She had almost stepped out in front of a car.

   _____

   _____

DAY 122

CAPITALIZATION:

1. " in 1880, kowee, a thingit indian chief, led prospectors along gaslinkau channel to gold creek," insisted will.

PUNCTUATION:

2. Marsha asked   Was Julius Caesar the famous Roman leader born in 100 B C

PARTS OF SPEECH: PRONOUNS

Objective pronouns are <u>me</u>, <u>him</u>, <u>her</u>, <u>us</u>, <u>them</u>, <u>whom</u>, <u>you</u>, and <u>it</u>.
Objective pronouns serve as objects: direct object
                                        indirect object
                                        object of the preposition

Write <u>D.O.</u> for direct object, <u>I.O.</u> for indirect object, and <u>O.P.</u> for object of the preposition:

3. A. _____ Uncle Ned gave **her** an old truck with a running board.
   B. _____ From **whom** did you receive the pendant?
   C. _____ Who chose **you** to be in charge?

PARTS OF SPEECH: VERBS

Circle the correct verb:

4. A. The driver removed the flat tire and (sat, set) the new one beside the car.
   B. Miriam has (laid, lain) several boards over a puddle by her front door.

SENTENCE COMBINING:

5. The company filed a lawsuit.
   The company is a catering company.
   The company claimed it had catered a party.
   The company claimed it had not been paid.

   _____

   _____

DAY 123

CAPITALIZATION:

1. during the reign of queen mary I, over three hundred english protestants were killed in britain.

PUNCTUATION:

2. Their son in laws company is located at 12 Oaksprig Lane Bakersfield CA 93313

PARTS OF SPEECH: ADVERBS
Circle the correct word:

3. A. Trevor didn't want (nobody, anybody) to question him about the incident.
   B. Please shut the door (tight, tightly).

PARTS OF SPEECH: VERBS

The progressive tense is formed by adding a form of *to be* to a present participle.
Present Progressive = *is, am,* or *are* + present participle
(is going, am going, or are going)
Past Progressive = *was* or *were* + present participle (was going or were going)
Future Progressive = *shall be* or *will be* + present participle
(shall be going or will be going)

Write the correct tense:

4. A. _____ A Papago **will be wearing** an intricately designed basket.
   B. _____ The knight **was wearing** a tunic of chain mail.

SENTENCE COMBINING:

5. The article was about people in advertising.
   It appeared in a women's business magazine.
   It said that the average female chief executive officer makes more than the average male chief executive officer.

_____

_____

DAY 124

CAPITALIZATION:

1. the russian king, vladimir, converted to christianity in order to marry anna, sister of byzantine emperor basil II.

PUNCTUATION:

2. The A D A* blasted the authors low carbohydrate food diet as unhealthy unproven and even possibly dangerous

*American Dietetic Association

ANTONYMS/SYNONYMS/HOMONYMS:

3. A. An antonym for simple is _____.
   B. A synonym for nervous is _____.
   C. A homonym for find is _____.

PARTS OF SPEECH:
Than is usually used with comparative adjectives or adverbs.
   Examples: **He is older than I.**   (adjective)
              That's easier said than done.   (adverb)
Then is usually an adverb telling when.
   Example: **Ron smiled; then, he shook my hand.**

Circle the correct word:

4. A. The child cuddled the puppy; (than, then), she handed him to her dad.
   B. Her left hand is stronger (than, then) her right hand.
   C. June likes Japanese food more (than, then) Chinese food.

SENTENCE COMBINING:

5. The hotel opened a business library for guests.
   The library has individual work stations.
   The library has high-speed data ports.

   _____

   _____

DAY 125

CAPITALIZATION:

1. ludwig van beethoven, the great german composer, studied under hayden, then the leading composer in vienna.

PUNCTUATION:

2. Arriving in New York in 95 Wyatt was hired by the Long Island Journal

FRIENDLY LETTERS/ENVELOPES:
Write your return address on this envelope:

3.
_____
      _____
      _____
      _____
                        _____
                        _____
                        _____
_____

PARTS OF SPEECH: ADJECTIVES
Circle any proper adjectives:

4. Joshua attended a Baptist convention with a Peruvian friend.

SENTENCE COMBINING:

5. A tuatara is a spiny reptile.
   It lives in New Zealand.
   It is the only living member of the Rhynchocephalian order.

_____

_____

DAY 126

CAPITALIZATION:

1. after leaving mt. horeb, the hebrew people camped at kadesh.

PUNCTUATION:

2. For the holiday season numerous twinkling multi colored lights had been placed in Glendales Murphy Park

PHRASES/CLAUSES:
Write <u>DC</u> if the group of words is a dependent clause; write <u>IC</u> if the group of words is an independent clause:

3. A. _____ A fringe was attached to the heavy burlap material
   B. _____ If the queen had been planning to visit Stonehenge
   C. _____ She cried

PARTS OF SPEECH: PRONOUNS
Circle the correct reflexive pronoun:

4. Luke can't finish mowing the meadow (hisself, himself).

SENTENCE COMBINING:

5. The company ran an advertisement in a national newspaper.
   It was a full-color ad.
   It advertised a body wash.

   _____

   _____

DAY 127

CAPITALIZATION:

1. "the mars polar lander sent up by nasa* in 1999 was lost," explained nathan.

*National Aeronautical Space Administration agency

PUNCTUATION:
Place a dash (the width of <u>M</u>) or parentheses ( ) to provide additional information. Place brackets [ ] to include information within parentheses.

2. Peggy Cass Bud Collyer and Kitty Carlisle what a fun team starred in To Tell the Truth a television show

DICTIONARY USAGE:
¹rill (ril) n. a very small brook
²rill (ril) v. to flow like a brook
³rill (ril) n. a channel made by a stream

3. A. The old painting showed a young lady sitting on a bank with her feet dangling in a **rill**. Which definition best fits the use of *rill* in this sentence? _____

   B. Write a sentence using *rill* as a verb.

   _____
   _____

PARTS OF SPEECH: VERBS
The perfect tense is formed by adding a form of *to have* to a past participle.
   Present Perfect = *has* or *have* + past participle
   Past Perfect = *had* + past participle
   Future Perfect = *shall have* or *will have* + past participle

Write the tense of the underlined verb phrase:

4. _____ Parker <u>will have finished</u> by noon.

SENTENCE COMBINING:

5. An Olympic gold medalist ran 100 meters.
   He ran 100 meters in 9.8 seconds.
   This time was the second fastest in the world.

   _____
   _____

DAY 128

CAPITALIZATION:

Capitalize this outline:

1. i. paragraph writing
      a. topic sentence
      b. relevant details
   ii. passage writing
      a. thesis statement
      b. conclusion

PUNCTUATION:

2. Jasons dad didnt marry until age thirty two and his mom was nearly thirty

PARTS OF SPEECH: VERBS

Circle the correct form:

3. A. Mrs. Lindner's purse had (fallen, fell) to the floor.
   B. Several people (rose, raised) to greet the senator.
   C. Nelly might have (did, done) an extra project for additional points.
   D. A severe wind (blew, blown) through the valley last night.
   E. The children (laid, lay) on the bed with their mother.

PARTS OF SPEECH: PRONOUNS

4. (Me and my cousin, My cousin and I) are alike in many ways.

SENTENCE COMBINING:

5. The couple will wed at Lake Tahoe.
   The couple will wed at a favorite spot in the woods.
   The wedding will be attended by family and a few friends.

   _____

   _____

DAY 129

CAPITALIZATION:

1. did san jose's theater present *uh-oh, here comes christmas*, robert fulghum's holiday memories?

PUNCTUATION:

2. When youre finished washing and waxing your motorcycle Ken Id like you to help me

PARTS OF SPEECH: NOUNS
   Write the possessive form:

3. A. the leadership of Sir Winston Churchill - _____

   B. a decision made by Canisa and Dory - _____

   C. two vehicles, one owned by Dave and the other owned by Ali - _____

   _____

SENTENCE TYPES:
   Write an imperative sentence:

4. _____

SENTENCE COMBINING:

5. The priest wore a chasuble.
   A chasuble is a sleeveless outer garment.
   The priest was performing a mass.

   _____

   _____

DAY 130

CAPITALIZATION:

1. be sure to visit open air observatory skywalk at the john haveat terminal on michigan avenue in chicago.

PUNCTUATION:

2. On Thursday May 20 1982 their mothers friend purchased his first home in Witchita Kansas

SENTENCES/FRAGMENTS/RUN-ONS:
Write <u>S</u> for sentence, <u>F</u> for fragment, and <u>R-O</u> for run-on:

3. A. ____ Because it's Friday.
   B. ____ Sit down.
   C. ____ A farm in Brady Hollow last night after the fireworks.
   D. ____ The designer felt the fabric, it was too stiff.

PARTS OF SPEECH: PRONOUNS
Circle the correct reflexive pronoun:

4. The sorority members are keeping this street litter-free (themselves, theirselves).

SENTENCE COMBINING:

5. Roy Rogers was a cowboy singer.
   Roy Rogers was also a television star.
   He had a famous horse.
   The horse's name was Trigger.

   _____

   _____

DAY 131

CAPITALIZATION:

1. "black canyon national park, located southwest of denver," stated julian, "was created by congress in 1999."

PUNCTUATION:

2. Pulled by two spirited horses the carriage wound its way down Mill Road around the lake district and up Fox Hill

ANALOGIES:
Complete this analogy:

3. bovine : cow :: feline : _____
   (a) cat   (b) feelings   (c) cud   (d) dog

PARTS OF SPEECH: PRONOUNS
Circle the correct pronoun:

4. One of the boys left (their, his) weights by the front door.

SENTENCE COMBINING:

5. A nene is a goose.
   It inhabits waterless uplands.
   It lives in the Hawaiian Islands.
   It is endangered.

   _____

   _____

DAY 132

CAPITALIZATION:

1. in 1935, *walk two moons* received the newberry award presented by the american library association.

PUNCTUATION:

2. Corey asked How many ands may I use in a simple sentence

PARTS OF SPEECH: NOUNS
   Write the plural of each noun:

3. A. wolf - _____   E. tress - _____

    B. pax - _____   F. zucchini - _____

    C. rally - _____   G. parley - _____

    D. parka - _____   H. torpedo - _____

PARTS OF SPEECH: PREPOSITIONS
   List thirty prepositions:

4. _____

   _____

SENTENCE COMBINING:

5. Brent is allergic to colognes and perfumes.
   Brent gets a headache.
   Brent's headache usually lasts several hours.

   _____

   _____

DAY 133

CAPITALIZATION:

1. "does your aunt," asked rosa, "always eat dover beach * sardines on an english muffin as an afternoon snack?"

*brand name

PUNCTUATION:

2. On Thursday December 9 1999 UNITY* held a fund raiser at an inn located at 5405 E Lincoln Drive

*abbreviation for United National Indian Tribal Youth

PARTS OF SPEECH: ADJECTIVES

Limiting adjectives don't describe; they modify (go over to) **a noun or pronoun. Circle any limiting adjectives:**

3. This unusual violin with no strings was found in the attic of an old farmhouse.

TEXT COMPONENTS:

   Predicate adjectives,   131, 329-335
   Predicate nominatives,   127, 268-271, 475, 478-479
   Prepositions,   3-71
       adverb vs. preposition,   41, 417-423
       definition,   12

Use the above index to answer these questions:

4. A. On which page does the unit on prepositions end? _____
   B. On how many pages will you find information about predicate nominatives? _____

SENTENCE COMBINING:

5. Blue Ridge is a range of the Appalachians.
   It extends from the South Mountains in Pennsylvania to northern Georgia.

   _____

   _____

DAY 134

CAPITALIZATION:

1. several years ago, uncle jack met vice-president al gore, a democrat, at a midwest conference.

PUNCTUATION:

2. Its not surprising I believe that those boys friend wrote an award winning essay

PARTS OF SPEECH:

Write *can* or *may*:

3. I know that you _____ climb the tree, but the park attendant said that you _____ not.

SPELLING:

Following a *c*, *a*, *u*, and *o* usually make the *c* say the *k* sound:
    cat   cut   cot

Following a *c*, *e*, *i*, and *y* usually make the *c* say the *s* sound:
    cent   cinder   cyst

If a word ending in *c* adds a suffix beginning with *e*, *i*, and *y*, the letter *k* is usually added to maintain the *k* sound.
    panic + ing = panicking

Circle the correct spelling:

4. A. trafficing   trafficking   C. metrical   metrickal
   B. panicky   panicy   D. picniced   picnicked

SENTENCE COMBINING:

5. Jina is squeezing lemons.
   She is making lemonade.
   Dave is squeezing oranges.
   He is making orange juice.

_____

_____

DAY 135

CAPITALIZATION:

1. according to the american association of poison control, rattlesnakes cause many bites in america.

PUNCTUATION:

2. Yes youll need to read the article entitled Herb News in Healthy Gardening magazine

PARTS OF SPEECH: ADJECTIVES
Circle the correct adjective form:

3. The boxer was (more sluggish, most sluggish) after the seventh round.

BUSINESS LETTERS/ENVELOPES:
Write your return address; then, address the envelope to Nista Enterprises, Inc. at Post Office Box 12520 in the city of Scottsdale in the state of Arizona. The zip code is 85255.

4.

SENTENCE COMBINING:

5. The children played in the woods for several hours.
   Then, they checked themselves for ticks.

DAY 136

CAPITALIZATION:

1. At marketmax supermarket, mother bought cobrite* toothpaste and a copy of <u>tuesday with morrie</u>.

*brand name

PUNCTUATION:

2. Although he is warm friendly and intelligent he tends to be too frugal   said Ann

PARTS OF SPEECH: NOUNS
Write the possessive form:

3. A. the British accent of their hostess - _____

   B. a weekly meeting for nurses - _____

   C. a townhouse belonging to Sam and Ann - _____

PARTS OF SPEECH:
An infinitive phrase can serve as a noun. It may serve as a subject or as a direct object.

   Examples: **To act on Broadway** is his dream.   subject
   I want **to go with you**.   direct object

Write S if the infinitive phrase serves as the subject; write DO if the infinitive phrase serves as a direct object:

4. A. _____   **To remain calm** was his goal.
   B. _____   They like **to go treasure hunting**.

SENTENCE COMBINING:

5. During a lightning storm, charges from the ground are emitted upward. They surge toward electrical charges in the clouds.

   _____

   _____

DAY 137

CAPITALIZATION:
Capitalize this part of a Emily Dickinson poem:

1. there is no frigate like a book

    to take us lands away,

    nor any coursers like a page

    of prancing poetry.

PUNCTUATION:

2. Cold and tired the traveler slowly walked over to the inns welcoming blazing fire

DICTIONARY: ALPHABETIZING
Place these words in alphabetical order:

   butane   butter   butler   butte   butcher   but

3. _____

PARTS OF SPEECH: NOUNS
Circle any nouns:

4. A harlequin is a character in comedy who has a masked face and an outfit with a pattern of dark and light diamonds.

SENTENCE COMBINING:

5. Roller coasters originated in Russia in the 1500's.
   Roller coasters were ice-covered wooden ramps.
   These wooden ramps were about 600 feet long.

   _____

   _____

DAY 138

CAPITALIZATION:

1. "was cyrus the great a leader of the persian empire?" asked representative lucas.

PUNCTUATION:

Punctuate this inside address and salutation of a business letter:

2. The Charity Foundation
   1 Banting Ln
   Lenox MA   01240

   Dear Madam

PARTS OF SPEECH: ADJECTIVES/ADVERBS
   Circle the correct word:

3. He always does that (easy, easily).

PARTS OF SPEECH: PRONOUNS
   Circle the correct pronoun:

4. A. My aunt is (her, she) in the long red satin gown.
   B. Please sit beside Travis and (I, me).
   C. The stern director handed Juan and (him, he) a lengthy script.
   D. (We, Us) students must buy special legal-sized note pads for history class.

SENTENCE COMBINING:

5. The town was located in a Mississippi River flood plain.
   The entire town had been flooded.
   The town voted to relocate to higher ground.

   _____

   _____

DAY 139

CAPITALIZATION:

1. "last autumn, the bryer family visited fisherman's wharf in san francisco," said jo.

PUNCTUATION:

2. Tuckers friend however doesnt like to bake a traditional two layer cake

PARTS OF SPEECH: CONJUNCTIONS

Choose the correct verb in this sentence containing correlative conjunctions.   Then, circle the correlative conjunctions:

3. A. Neither the principal nor the teachers (eat, eats) in the cafeteria.

   B. Neither the teachers nor the principal (eat, eats) a full lunch.

LIBRARY SKILLS:

4. A. A book of words and their synonyms is a _____.

   B. A _____ is a notation for the reader to refer to another article or book with similar information.

   C. A story written by a person discussing his or her own life is a(an) _____.

SENTENCE COMBINING:

5. The Homestead Act of 1862 drew many people to Nebraska.
   Many veterans of the Civil War went there to live.
   Many immigrants went there to live.
   The immigrants were Scandinavian, Irish, German, Czech, and Slovakian.

   _____

   _____

DAY 140

CAPITALIZATION:

1. charles carrol who had signed the declaration of independence in 1776 laid the first stone of the baltimore and ohio railroad in 1828.

PUNCTUATION:

2. They moved from Butler County Pennsylvania to a tropical island said Maj Scott

PARTS OF SPEECH: PRONOUNS

Nominative pronouns are *I, he, she, we, they, who, you,* and *it*. Nominative pronouns serve as the subject or the predicate nominative of a sentence.

If the nominative pronoun is serving as a subject, write S; if the nominative pronoun is serving as a predicate nominative, write PN:

3. A. _____ Has **she** seen the antique Italian console table?
   B. _____ The last museum visitors were **they** in a double-decker bus.
   C. _____ The finalists are Dan, Elizabeth, and **I**.

ANTONYMS/SYNONYMS/HOMONYMS:

4. A. A synonym for send is _____.
   B. A homonym for alter is _____.
   C. An antonym for chaos is _____.

SENTENCE COMBINING:

5. Coney Island was a popular spot in the 1880's.
   Coney Island is a section of Brooklyn, New York.
   It had beaches and boardwalks.

   _____

   _____

DAY 141

CAPITALIZATION:

1. they attended st. michael's cathedral, a russian church located on lincoln street in sitka, alaska.

PUNCTUATION:

2. On Sept 25 1789 Pres James Monroe introduced twelve constitutional amendments to our countrys government plan

SENTENCES/FRAGMENTS/RUN-ONS:

Change this run-on sentence to an acceptable one:

3. She studied the map, then she drew a red line between Keene and Dublin.

_____

FRIENDLY LETTERS/ENVELOPES:

(A) _____
(B) _____
(C) _____
(D) _____
(E) _____

Write the parts of a friendly letter:

4. A. _____   D. _____
   B. _____   E. _____
   C. _____

SENTENCE COMBINING:

5. A silkworm is a moth.
   Its larva spins a large amount of silk in building its cocoon.

_____

_____

DAY 142

CAPITALIZATION:

1. last night, lani flew from mc carren international airport to the tip of baja peninsula on the sea of cortez.

PUNCTUATION:

2. Wow At a sports center in Tulsa Oklahoma STAR* equipment is used   exclaimed Ty

*acronym for Sports Training and Rehabilitation

PARTS OF SPEECH: ADJECTIVES
   Circle any adjectives:

3. An edible fat from the fruit of several palm trees can be used to make fragrant soap and various lubricating greases.

PARTS OF SPEECH:
   Circle the correct word:

4. A. The hotel receptionist answered, "(Your, You're) welcome."
   B. A rat retraced (it's, its) path along the dirt trail.
   C. Will you please give me (there, their, they're) new address?
   D. Kosey wants to discuss his test grade, (to, two, too).

SENTENCE COMBINING:

5. Buccaneers preyed on Spanish ships in the 1600's.
   Buccaneers also preyed on Spanish settlements during this time.
   These settlements were in the West Indies.

_____

_____

DAY 143

CAPITALIZATION:

1. "citizenship day," explained miss levy, "is a combination of two former special days, "constitution day" and "i am an american day."

PUNCTUATION:

Punctuate this friendly letter:

2.
                                         1 E Briar Road
                                         Oak Ridge TN 37830
                                         Aug 7 20--

Dear Devi
      Did you find enough information on da Vinci What an interesting man   I learned that he painted the Mona Lisa plus made sketches of submarines and airplanes

                                           See ya
                                           Shelby

PARTS OF SPEECH: NOUNS

3. Is *beauty* an abstract or concrete noun? _____

COMPOUND/COMPLEX/COMPOUND-COMPLEX SENTENCES:

A compound-complex sentence has two or more independent (main) clauses and one or more dependent (subordinate) clauses.

    Example: <u>Maggie twisted her foot</u>, but <u>she managed to limp to the dugout</u>
                   independent clause   *independent clause*
           <u>although her foot throbbed with pain.</u>
              dependent clause

Place a √ before a compound-complex sentence:

4. A. _____ Maggie grinned, but she didn't move until her mom motioned to her.

   B. _____ Caleb's mother snacked on pretzels as she prepared dinner.

SENTENCE COMBINING:

5. The department store elevator door opened only a foot.
   The shoppers in the elevator did not panic.

_____

_____

DAY 144

CAPITALIZATION:

1. during cheyenne frontier days, we watched the u. s. a. f. thunderbirds and attended an open house at f. e. warren air force base.

PUNCTUATION:
Puncutate these titles:

2. A. The Diary (short story)
   B. Visiting the South (newspaper article)
   C. Working with Tile (video)
   D. This Is My Desire (song)
   E. Flowers and Ferns (magazine)

PARTS OF SPEECH: VERBS
Circle the correct verb:

3. Everyone of the employees (has, have) asked for a raise.

PARTS OF SPEECH: PRONOUNS
Circle the correct pronoun:

4. You seem to be taller than (I, me).

SENTENCE COMBINING

5. A hurricane dumped twenty inches of water.
   The hurricane was named Floyd.
   A previous hurricane had passed through a few weeks earlier.
   The ground was already saturated.

_____

_____

DAY 145

CAPITALIZATION:

1. <u>jackie: behind the myth</u> was an interesting documentary about jacqueline kennedy, the wife of president john f. kennedy.

PUNCTUATION:

2. Carol Brant R N stated with authority Use sunblock Dont stay in the sun too long

PARTS OF SPEECH: INTERJECTIONS
Write a sentence containing an interjection:

3. _____

PARTS OF SPEECH: PRONOUNS
Circle the correct pronoun:

4. Marcia and (them, they) are going to the river this weekend.

SENTENCE COMBINING:

5. Mr. and Mrs. Gund want to buy a home.
    They made an appointment with a real estate agent.
    The real estate agent is a friend of Mr. Gund's grandfather.
    Mr. and Mrs. Gund want a small home in the country.

    _____

    _____

DAY 146

CAPITALIZATION:

1. scientists have discovered an ancient coastline under the black sea; this offers evidence of a great flood, the possible source of the *old testament* story of noah.

PUNCTUATION:

2. Its raining Patti shouted Will someone loan me an umbrella

DICTIONARY: GUIDE WORDS
Place a √ before a word that will appear on the same dictionary page as the words <u>soft-shell</u> and <u>solder</u>:

3. A. ___ soffit   C. ___ soldier   E. ___ soilless   G. ___ sojourn
   B. ___ soft-spoken D. ___ soldan   F. ___ solace   H. ___ solemn

BUSINESS LETTERS/ENVELOPES:
There are many variations to a business letter. Use this model in labeling the parts. Remember that a business letter also has an inside address, a printed signature, and a written signature.

(A) _____
(B) _____
(C) _____
(D) _____
(E) _____
(F)
(G) _____

Label the parts of the business letter:

4. A. _____   E. _____
   B. _____   F. _____
   C. _____   G. _____
   D. _____

SENTENCE COMBINING:

5. In 1904, tenor opera singer Enrico Caruso made his first recording. The Victor Company recorded it on a ten inch record disk.

_____

_____

DAY 147

CAPITALIZATION:
Capitalize this friendly letter:

1.
                                                           2 horn road
                                                          belmont nh   03320
                                                          feb 12 20--

my dear friend
    have you been to oak creek canyon   this area of the southwest is beautiful
    were hoping to visit you on april 14   did you know that is pan american day
                                                                  truly yours
                                                                  victoria

PUNCTUATION:

2. Punctuate the above friendly letter.

PARTS OF SPEECH: NOUNS
Circle any proper nouns in the following sentence:

3. LAST JULY, JAN AND HER DAD HIKED THE ALPS MOUNTAINS IN EUROPE.

PARTS OF SPEECH: PRONOUNS
Write a sentence containing a reflexive pronoun:

4. _____

SENTENCE COMBINING:

5. The Luminere brothers produced movies of ordinary outdoor activities.
   They lost audiences to other producers.
   These producers used comedy and drama.

_____

_____

DAY 148

CAPITALIZATION:

1. in 1960, governor rockefeller of new york set aside september 23 as american indian day to honor native americans.

PUNCTUATION:

Write the abbreviation:

2. A. Saint Paul - _____   E. Mount Hood - _____
   B. August - _____   F. Monday - _____
   C. centimeter - _____   G. 54th Place - _____
   D. Nebraska - _____

SPELLING:

Following a **c**, *e* usually makes the **c** say the *s* sound: trance
Following a **g**, *e* usually makes the **g** say the *j* sound: large
If a word ending in **c** adds *able*, the letter **e** is usually maintained to make the **c** say the *s* sound.
   Example: trace + **able** = trac**e**able
If a word ending in **g** adds *able*, the letter **e** is usually maintained to make the **g** say the *j* sound.
   Example: change + **able** = chang**e**able

Circle the correct spelling:

3. A. enforceable   enforcable   C. manageable   managable
   B. debateable   debatable   D. deploreable deplorable

PARTS OF SPEECH: VERBS

Write a sentence containing an infinitve:

4. _____

SENTENCE COMBINING:

5. John Singer Sargent first drew attention at a Royal Academy art show.
   He had begun painting portraits nearly thirty years earlier.

_____

_____

DAY 149

CAPITALIZATION:
Capitalize these titles:

1. A. "satelite radio is on the horizon"

   B. a first look at spiders

   C. "do all the good you can"

   D. seashells in my pocket

PUNCTUATION:

2. Vinton G Cerf Father of the Internet has been likened to a modern day Gutenburg

PHRASES/CLAUSES:
Write P if the group of words is a phrase. Write DC if the group of words is a dependent clause; write IC if the group of words is an independent clause:

3. A. _____ Tripping over a shoe

   B. _____ When I tripped over a shoe

   C. _____ I tripped over a shoe

PARTS OF SPEECH: VERBS
Circle the correct verb:

4. The baby (lies, lays) on his tummy to sleep.

SENTENCE COMBINING:

5. The Hope Diamond weighs 44.5 carats.
   It was purchased by a family in the early 1900's.
   The wife wanted to wear it as a head ornament.

   _____

   _____

DAY 150

CAPITALIZATION:

1. named by philip of macedonia, philippi was the site of the battle of actium in 33 b.c.

PUNCTUATION:

2. The Britannic a ship was sunk off the coast of Greece on Nov 21 1916 few passengers died

PARTS OF SPEECH:

An infinitive phrase can serve as a noun. It can be an appositive or a predicate nominative.

Examples: His wish, **to visit the President**, had been granted. *appositive*
Her goal is **to become a jockey**. *predicate nominative*

Circle any infinitve phrase. Write APP. if the infinitive phrase serves as an appositive and P.N. if the infinitive phrase serves as a predicate nominative:

3. A. _____ They met the baby's demand, to be fed immediately.
   B. _____ My desire is to be as patient as you.

PHRASES AND CLAUSES:

Circle the dependent clause:

4. After the choir sang four lively selections, Reverend Harris preached a sermon.

SENTENCE COMBINING:

5. Jean Henri Dunant was a Swiss philanthropist.
   He helped to start the Red Cross.
   He had seen wounded soldiers left on battlefields in Austria in 1859.

_____

_____

DAY 151

CAPITALIZATION:

1. the musical, *the sound of music*, by rogers and hammerstein, opened on broadway in 1959.

PUNCTUATION:
Punctuate the following:

2. A. Regis Express   (name of a train)
   B. The Evening Post   (newspaper)
   C. Greed   (name of a television game show)
   D. Word Problem Solving   (title of a chapter)
   E. Cattle Country   (magazine)

ANALOGIES:
Complete this analogy:

3. spider : arachnid :: snail : _____
   (a) slow   (b) science   (c) mollusk   (d) vertebrate

PARTS OF SPEECH: NOUNS
Circle any appositives:

4. *A Pueblo Chief on His Favorite Buffalo Horse*, an oil on canvas, was painted in 1853 by John Mix Stanley, an American explorer and artist.

SENTENCE COMBINING:

5. On March 24, 1900, there was a ceremony in New York City.
   The mayor shoveled a scoop of dirt for the first New York subway.
   The mayor was Van Wyct.
   The subway would connect Manhattan and Brooklyn.

   _____

   _____

DAY 152

CAPITALIZATION:

1. "is coastal airlines the official airlines for the new york city marathon and the new york yankees?" asked kayla.

PUNCTUATION:

Place a dash (the width of M) or parentheses ( ) to provide additional information. Place brackets [ ] to include information within parentheses.

2. Kerry likes your idea but I dont feel that mens plastic raincoats will sell at least not in the Southwest

PARTS OF SPEECH: PRONOUNS

Objective pronouns are me, him, her, us, them, whom, you, and it.
Objective pronouns serve as objects: direct object
                                        indirect object
                                        object of the preposition

Write D.O. for direct object, I.O. for indirect object, and O.P. for object of the preposition:

3. A. _____ A guide showed **them** a picture of a grizzly bear.
   B. _____ Jeb put down the box and sat on **it**.
   C. _____ His mother admonished **him** not to be late again?

PARTS OF SPEECH: VERBS

Underline the verb phrase and write the tense:

4. A. _____ Micah had enrolled in a cooking class.
   B. _____ Tara has bought a motorcycle.

SENTENCE COMBINING:

5. The teddy bear toy was inspired by Theodore Roosevelt.
   President Roosevelt refused to kill a bear cub during a hunting expedition.

   _____

   _____

DAY 153

CAPITALIZATION:

1. "did you know," asked carlo, "that <u>voyager I</u> traveled near saturn in 1980?"

PUNCTUATION:

2. Brad used to live in St Croix however he now lives at 2 Creamery Rd Oswego NY

DICTIONARY USAGE:

bow (bau) v. 1: to stop competing 2: to lower the head, body, or knee
bow (bau) n. the forward part of a ship
bow (bo) n. 1: something bent into a curve 2: a weapon made with a bent piece and string 3: a metal ring or loop 4: a knot formed by looping ribbon
bow (bo) v. 1: to bend into a curve 2: to play a musical instrument with a bow

3. A. Words that are spelled alike but sound differently are called *homographs*. Write the pronunciation of the homograph that is similar to the sound a dog makes (*bow* wow). _____

    B. He detached his key from the bow and handed it to his friend.

    Which definition best fits the use of *bow (bo)* used as a noun in the above sentence? _____

PARTS OF SPEECH: PRONOUNS
Circle the reflexive pronoun; box its antecedent:

4. The cheerleaders want to plan a pep rally themselves.

SENTENCE COMBINING:

5. The first continental car race was in 1903.
   Tom Fetch drove a Packard.
   It took him fifty-one days to travel across the country.

_____

_____

DAY 154

CAPITALIZATION:

1. in argentina, i crossed the strait of magellan and picnicked at cabo domingo, a fossil hunting site.

PUNCTUATION:

2. Are you familiar with this book by Chiko Tang a financial expert   asked the manager

PARTS OF SPEECH: VERBS

Cross out any prepositional phrase(s). Underline the subject once and the verb/verb phrase twice:

3. A.   After their wedding, chimes (rang, rung) for five minutes.

   B.   Hasn't the President's wife (wore, worn) gloves on several occasions?

   C.   During the storm, Mom had (gave, given) extra flashlights to our neighbors.

PARTS OF SPEECH: ADJECTIVES

Circle any proper adjectives; box any predicate adjectives:

4. His stay in a French country home was fun and relaxing.

SENTENCE COMBINING:

5. Mr. and Mrs. Lane went to a movie.
   They saw a romantic comedy.
   Mr. Lane thought it was funny.
   Mrs. Lane thought it was boring.

_____

_____

DAY 155

CAPITALIZATION:

1. recordings for the blind and dyslexic* was founded in 1948 for blinded world war II veterans attending college.

*a non-profit organization

PUNCTUATION:

2. Whenever our dad makes barbecued pork he uses Chans Soul Food Cookbook

PARTS OF SPEECH: ADJECTIVES/ADVERBS
Circle the correct word:

3. The child had behaved (bad, badly) during the service.

SENTENCES/FRAGMENTS/RUN-ONS:
Write S for sentence, F for fragment, and R-O for run-on:

4. A. ____ Ready for action, the soccer player leaned forward.
    B. ____ Sand used to make glass.
    C. ____ Her high heels clicked on the pavement as she dashed across the street.
    D. ____ Give me your hand I'll help you.

SENTENCE COMBINING:

5. Conservationists did not want to paint the antique door with new paint.
    They chemically removed the old paint.
    They reapplied the old paint.

    _____

    _____

DAY 156

CAPITALIZATION:

1. in 1833, supreme court chief justice john marshall and other washingtonians formed the washington national monument society.

PUNCTUATION:

2. Located near Cameo Beach that hotel has seventy five rooms with views of the ocean the village or the gardens

PARTS OF SPEECH: VERBS

Remember: The progressive tense is formed by adding a form of *to be* to a present participle.

Write the tense:

3. A. _____ The infant developed a rash on his forehead.
   B. _____ Kim is studying at a beauty academy.
   C. _____ Bonaire is an island in the Netherland Antilles.
   D. _____ A goldsmith has designed an oval filigree pin.

PARTS OF SPEECH: PRONOUNS

Write S. for subject, P.N. for predicate nominative, D.O. for direct object, I.O. for indirect object, and O.P. for object of the preposition:

4. A. _____ A parking attendant asked **her** for her keys.
   B. _____ Their favorite cousins are Anders and **he**.
   C. _____ By **whom** were you sitting?

SENTENCE COMBINING:

5. The waiter served a turban of sole.
   A turban is a stuffed fillet of fish.

   _____

   _____

DAY 157

CAPITALIZATION:

1. in speech 101, a student pretended to feed brasco* pecan cookies to a rabbit during her presentation entitled "know what is good for your pet."

*brand name

PUNCTUATION:

2. When youre placing your order please ask for the following extra ketchup a side of ranch dressing and a glass of water

PARTS OF SPEECH: PRONOUNS
Circle the correct pronoun:

3. A. The architect and (us, we) will be meeting about the building.
   B. The winners were the Lundts and (us, we).
   C. (We, Us) Americans cannot take our freedoms for granted.

PARTS OF SPEECH: ADVERBS/ADJECTIVES
Circle the correct word:

4. Don't walk so (slow, slowly).

SENTENCE COMBINING:

5. O. Henry was a famous short-story writer.
   O. Henry was an American.
   O. Henry was a pseudonym for William Sydney Porter.

_____

_____

DAY 158

CAPITALIZATION:

1. the decent docent doesn't doze:
   he teaches standing on his toes.
   his students dassn't doze and does,
   and that's what teaching is and was.

   -david mc cord, american writer

PUNCTUATION:

2. Beginning January 31 2001 Travelo Airways began flying from Sacramento to Athens Greece

PARTS OF SPEECH: ADVERBS
   Circle the correct form:

3. Grandmother smiled (more beautifully, most beautifully) for the third picture.

PARTS OF SPEECH:

   Write <u>N</u> if the boldfaced word serves as a noun, <u>A</u> if the word serves as an adjective, and <u>V</u> if the word serves as a verb:

4. A. _____ Her suit was navy blue with a white **shawl** collar.
   B. _____ Have you seen a fan-shaped **shawl**?
   C. _____ The boy **shawled** his books in his jacket as he dashed into the rain.

SENTENCE COMBINING:

5. Jane Canary's nickname was Calamity Jane.
   She was nicknamed this because she had helped so many people in distress.
   She had been a scout for General Custer.

   _____

   _____

DAY 159

CAPITALIZATION:

1. in my sociology class at harrisburg area college, i studied the effects of the stock market crash on american society.

PUNCTUATION:

2. An antique lover Mrs Majeski purchased Restoring Heirlooms a book about repairing old furniture

PARTS OF SPEECH: CONJUNCTIONS

3. A. *And, but,* and *or* are called _____ conjunctions.
    B. *Both-and, either-or,* and *neither-nor* are called _____ conjunctions.

TEXT COMPONENTS:

TYPES OF SENTENCES... 373
SENTENCES, FRAGMENTS, AND RUN-ONS.................. 379
PHRASES AND CLAUSES.. 387
ADVERBS... 393
    Defined, 393
    Adverbs that tell *how*, 397
    Adverbs that tell *where*, 405

Use this table of contents to answer the following questions:

4. A. The chapter concerning sentence types begins on which page? _____
    B. To which page will you turn to find materials relating to adverbs telling *how*? _____
    C. The chapter about phrases and clauses ends on page _____.

SENTENCE COMBINING:

5. Lenny arrived home first.
    Terry followed him.
    Luis came next.

    _____

    _____

DAY 160

CAPITALIZATION:

1. during a campaign in burma in world war II, field marshal william slim led the british forces.

PUNCTUATION:

2. After sixteen years of searching he found the Nuestra Senora de Atocha* in fifty five feet of water off Key West Florida

*name of a ship

PARTS OF SPEECH: PRONOUNS
Circle the correct pronoun:

3. A. Nessa and (them, they) are building a canoe.
   B. The boat captain handed the fishermen and (she, her) a travel plan.
   C. "With (whom, who) are you traveling to India?" asked Mrs. Garza.
   D. "Don't trust (them, those) old broken stairs," suggested Tad.

PARTS OF SPEECH: NOUNS
Circle the gerund phrase:

4. Bonnie and her friend enjoyed traveling to Mexico City.

SENTENCE COMBINING:

5. Molly won a stuffed toy at a fair.
   It was a dinosaur.
   The dinosaur was purple.
   She had thrown three rings on a bottle.
   The bottle was glass.

   _____

   _____

DAY 161

CAPITALIZATION:

1. when we visited tangier island in the chesapeake bay, we attended swain methodist church near mailboat harbor.

PUNCTUATION:

2. Its unsinkable   exclaimed the proud builders of the Titanic which sank on April 14 1912 during its maiden voyage

PARTS OF SPEECH: NOUNS
Write the plural of each noun:

3. A. buoy - _____   E. gulf - _____

   B. ebony - _____   F. zero - _____

   C. typhoon - _____   G. topaz - _____

   D. patch - _____   H. clergywoman - _____

PARTS OF SPEECH: PREPOSITIONS
List forty prepositions:

4. _____

   _____

   _____

SENTENCE COMBINING:

5. The first full length comedy starred Charlie Chaplin.
   It was entitled <u>Tillies Pinctured Romance</u>.
   Chaplin later became a writer and director.

   _____

   _____

DAY 162

CAPITALIZATION:

1. martin luther who started the reformation in europe received his degree from the university of wittenburg.

PUNCTUATION:

2. After Auguste Ottos invention of a four stroke engine Karl Benz built a practical marketable car

DICTIONARY: ALPHABETIZING

Place these words in alphabetical order:

conversation   converse   conversable
conversant   conversationalist   conversation piece

3. _____
   _____

PARTS OF SPEECH: ADJECTIVES

Circle the correct adjective form:

4. Your third choice seems (more realistic, most realistic).

SENTENCE COMBINING:

5. A French scientist successfully tested an anti-rabies vaccine.
   The year was 1885.
   The scientist's name was Louis Pasteur.
   The vaccine was tested on a boy.
   The boy had been bitten by an infected dog.

   _____
   _____

DAY 163

CAPITALIZATION:

1. "his uncle usually plays the french horn," said rita, "each year at the mardi gras in new orleans."

PUNCTUATION:

2. Even though Thomas A Edisons teacher thought him to be retarded Thomas patented more than 1000 inventions in his lifetime

PARTS OF SPEECH:
Circle the correct word:

3. A. What is the (affect, effect) of soil erosion on plants?
   B. (There, Their, They're) planning a huge party.
   C. Is (your, you're) apartment on the second floor?
   D. Les, (can, may) we take our surfboards along to the beach?
   E. I believe that (its, it's) necessary to respond to a R.S.V.P.

LIBRARY SKILLS:

4. A. A list of works referred to in a text (book or research paper) and placed at the end of the text is called a _____.

   B. A _____ dictionary provides information regarding famous people.

SENTENCE COMBINING:

5. Helen Keller lost her sight and hearing at the age of two due to illness.
   Anne Sullivan taught her to read by Braille.
   Anne Sullivan taught her to converse by touch.
   Anne Sullivan taught her to write using a special typewriter.

   _____

   _____

DAY 164

CAPITALIZATION:

1. does flemish refer to the people of belgium, a country bordering on the north sea?

PUNCTUATION:

Punctuate this business letter:

2. March 4 20--

   Proot Corporation Inc
   P O Box 1
   Lawrence KS   66044

   Dear Madam

   Having used many of Proots products for twenty one years Id like to say that I like your terry slippers best

   Sincerely

   Bibi Dosort

PARTS OF SPEECH:

Circle the correct word:

3. His mother weighs scarcely more (than, then) a hundred pounds.

SPELLING:

A two syllable word that ends in consonant-vowel-consonant and whose accent is on the second syllable will often double the final consonant when adding a suffix beginning with a vowel.
   Example: begin = be **gin´** = be **gin´** + ing = **beginning**

4. Add *ing* to *forget*: _____

SENTENCE COMBINING:

5. Harriet Quimby was the first American woman to earn a pilot's license.
   Mme. Dutrie of France was the first woman in the world to receive a pilot's license.

   _____

   _____

DAY 165

CAPITALIZATION:

1. "have you, mom," asked alec, "seen the pictures of our memorial day trip to that colorado dude ranch?"

PUNCTUATION:

2. Enrico Fermi Ph D designer of the nuclear reactor first developed a theory concerning the behavior of electrons protons and neutrons

ANTONYMS/SYNONYMS/HOMONYMS:

3. A. A homonym for real is _____.
   B. An antonym for confused is _____.
   C. A synonym for rare is _____.

COMPOUND/COMPLEX/COMPOUND-COMPLEX SENTENCES:
A compound-complex sentence has two or more independent (main) clauses and one or more dependent (subordinate) clauses.

   Example: A tour guide led the group, but she answered few questions
                      independent clause   *independent clause*
              because she spoke little German.
                      dependent clause

Place a √ before a compound-complex sentence:

4. A. _____ Although she tried diligently, Erica couldn't grab onto the rope.
   B. _____ After he was in the army, Lance studied law, and he later joined his father's firm.

SENTENCE COMBINING:

5. Reverend William Booth had a church called Christian Mission Church.
   He was told it seemed like a volunteer army.
   He renamed it the Salvation Army.

   _____

   _____

DAY 166

CAPITALIZATION:

1. they saw the play, <u>macbeth</u>, performed by the lyric opera company in chicago last december.

PUNCTUATION:

2. Miss Coe my guitar instructor lives at 56 E Regal Lane McKnightstown PA   17310

SENTENCE TYPES:

Write a declarative sentence; then, change it to an interrogative one:

3. A. declarative - _____
   _____

   B. interrogative - _____
   _____

PARTS OF SPEECH: NOUNS

Write the possessive form:

4. A. a lantern shared by campers - _____
   B. books belonging to his grandfather - _____

SENTENCE COMBINING:

5. George Herman "Babe" Ruth is considered a great home run hitter.
   He played for the New York Yankees.
   Before he played for the Yankees, he played for the Red Sox.

   _____
   _____

DAY 167

CAPITALIZATION:

1. their friend won a new sports car at the arizona leukemia cup regatta held january 22 at lake pleasant.

PUNCTUATION:
Punctuate this friendly letter:

2.
                                              12222 Lewis Center Rd
                                              Westerville OH 43082
                                              Oct 1 20--

Dear Hayden
      Did you know that alcohol is terrible for your system in many ways Besides what weve learned about it affecting the brain its a toxin In fact it raises levels of cortisol a hormone that appears to send fat to the tummy area
                                                      Always
                                                      Seana

PARTS OF SPEECH: VERBS

3. A helping verb is also called a(an) _____ verb.

COMPOUND/COMPLEX/COMPOUND-COMPLEX SENTENCES:
Write **C** if the sentence is compound, write **CX** if the sentence is complex, and write **C-C** if the sentence is compound-complex:

4. A. _____ After Ty and his family moved to Ajo, we didn't hear from them again.
   B. _____ Dr. Noor bandaged my hand, but he didn't take Xrays.
   C. _____ The man who bought our car took out a loan, and he paid us in cash.

SENTENCE COMBINING:

5. Louis Chevrolet was born in Switzerland.
He was known as a daredevil in auto racing.
He later started an automobile company.

_____

_____

DAY 168

CAPITALIZATION:

1. a statue of augustus caesar, leader of the roman empire who died in 14 a.d., is located in the vatican.

PUNCTUATION:

2. Born in Huntingdon England Oliver Cromwell a Puritan farmer led forces against Britains king

DICTIONARY USAGE:

^{1}**primo** (prē mō) *n.* the first or leading part
^{2}**primo** (prē mō) *adv.* in the first place
^{3}**primo** (prē mō) *adj.* slang usage: of the finest quality

Write the part of speech used in each sentence:

3. A. Well, primo, you must understand my dislike for goat cheese. _____
   B. This drink is a primo blend of spices and cider. _____
   C. In the duet performance, she is the primo. _____

SPELLING:

A two syllable word that ends in consonant-vowel-consonant and whose accent is on the second syllable will often double the final consonant when adding a suffix beginning with a vowel.
Example: **regret** = **re gret´** = **re gret´ + able = regrettable**

4. Add *ed* to *omit:* _____

SENTENCE COMBINING:

5. In 1992, there were 5.4 billion people on Earth.
   This was twice as many as in 1952.
   _____
   _____

DAY 169

CAPITALIZATION:

1. the swiss philosopher, jean-jacques rousseau, wrote ideas that influenced the french revolution.

PUNCTUATION:

Punctuate the following titles:

2. A. Jack Frost   (video)
    B. Adventures in Space   (chapter title)
    C. You Can Do It   (essay)
    D. The Bucks Start Here   (book)
    E. Over the Rainbow   (song)
    F. Travel the Globe   (television show)

ANALOGIES:

Complete this analogy:

3. elucidate : enlighten :: muted : _____.
    (a) mutation   (b) subdued   (c) tones   (d) raucous

SENTENCES/FRAGMENTS/RUN-ONS:

Write S for sentence, F for fragment, and R-O for run-on:

4. A. ____ Tim pressed the lever, the bread popped out of the toaster.
    B. ____ Surrounded, the thief to the ground without making a sound.
    C. ____ Spaghettini is a pasta that's thinner than spaghetti but thicker than vermicelli.

SENTENCE COMBINING:

5. In the 1949 World Series, the Yankees won.
    They defeated the Brooklyn Dodgers.
    Jackie Robinson was voted Most Valuable Player.
    Jackie Robinson was a Dodger.

_____

_____

DAY 170

CAPITALIZATION:

1. the british under general robert ross burned the presidential mansion* and the united states capitol.

*building later named the White House

PUNCTUATION:

2. Yes you most definitely may speak with Kerrys mother about the odd incident Jean

PARTS OF SPEECH: VERBS

Write the verb phrase and the tense of this sentence:

By noon, the volunteers will have addressed thirty invitations to the charity auction.

3. A. Verb phrase: _____
   B. Verb tense: _____

TEXT COMPONENTS:

Antecedents, 501-505
Appositives, 273-275
Apostrophes, 575-579
Auxiliary verbs, 26, 88
Business letters, 661-662
   envelopes, 662

Use this index to answer the following questions:

4. A. On how many pages can information about appositives be found? _____
   B. On how many pages can information about auxiliary verbs be found? _____
   C. To which page will you turn to find how to address a business envelope? ___

SENTENCE COMBINING:

5. Corn was once the most valuable product in the United States.
   It was worth more than all the gold, silver, and bullion in America.

_____

_____

DAY 171

CAPITALIZATION:

1. the "it's about medicine" section of <u>the medical times</u> related that mayo clinic researchers believe that sinusitis is caused by a fungus.

PUNCTUATION:

2. Im preparing cornbread therefore hand me two eggs and one half cup of milk please

PARTS OF SPEECH: VERBS
Write the past participle form for the following verbs:

3. A. to drive - _____   E. to lay - _____
   B. to swim - _____   F. to see - _____
   C. to teach - _____   G. to rise - _____
   D. to run - _____   H. to drink - _____

COMPOUND/COMPLEX/COMPOUND-COMPLEX SENTENCES:

Write <u>C</u> if the sentence is compound, write <u>CX</u> if the sentence is complex, and write <u>C-C</u> if the sentence is compound-complex:

4. A. _____ Although a storm had been forecast, we packed our lunch and went fishing in a nearby bay.
   B. _____ The senator stood up, but she only nodded to the visitor.
   C. _____ A motorist asked for directions, but the farmer didn't respond until he had herded his sheep safely off the road.

SENTENCE COMBINING:

5. Thomas Nashe claimed that he introduced <u>ize</u> into the English language.
   He used the suffix to turn a noun into a verb.

_____

_____

DAY 172

CAPITALIZATION:

1. "edward jenner, an english doctor," said professor logan, "developed a vaccine to prevent small pox."

PUNCTUATION:

2. Their homeowners association met on Tuesday January 11 1999 to discuss architectural regulations

PARTS OF SPEECH: PRONOUNS
Circle the correct pronoun:

3. A. Dan has changed the oil in the car (hisself, himself).
   B. The bridesmaids are Nadia, Carla, and (me, I).
   C. Hand (we, us) crew members the rope.
   D. Several journalists spoke with the jurists (themselves, theirselves).

SPELLING:
Circle the correct spelling:

4. A. fameous   famous   F. manageable   managable
   B. shiping   shipping   G. interchangeable interchangable
   C. shipment   shippment   H. desirable   desireable
   D. releif   relief   I. decieves   deceives
   E. lonely   lonly   J. panicking   panicing

SENTENCE COMBINING:

5. Theodore Roosevelt was a President.
   He was the first President ever to leave the United States or its territories.
   He went to the Panama Canal for twelve days.
   He went on a ship.

_____

_____

DAY 173

CAPITALIZATION:

1. william t. g. morton who introduced the use of anesthetic in surgery, attended baltimore college of dental surgery.

PUNCTUATION:

2. No the mayors bid for re election wasnt successful but he may try again in two years

PHRASES/CLAUSES:

Write **P** if the group of words is a phrase. Write **DC** if the group of words is a dependent clause; write **IC** if the group of words is an independent clause:

3. A. _____ Delighted with the results
   B. _____ After she began to search for the lost dog
   C. _____ Having been outside in the cold for an hour
   D. _____ After lunch in a park, we went to a museum.

DIFFICULT WORDS:

Circle the correct word:

4. A. (There's, Theirs) a different time zone in Hawaii.
   B. "This tape is designed (to, too, two) relax you," said the store clerk.
   C. "(Your, You're) actions reflect your thoughts," warned the instructor.
   D. Gary and she are going (there, their, they're) next summer.
   E. "(It's, Its) not wise to stay outside during a hurricane," she remarked.

SENTENCE COMBINING:

5. He is proud of his Dutch ancestry.
   He is determined to trace his ancestry back to the 1600's.
   He is researching his family tree.

   _____

   _____

DAY 174

CAPITALIZATION:

1. when queen isabella married king ferdinand, they captured granada, the only spanish kingdom to be under moslem rule.

PUNCTUATION:

2. Cross the t in tire Annie and edit your thesis statement again remarked Joey

PARTS OF SPEECH:

- *euphemism* - noun: the substitution of a pleasant expression for one that may offend
- *euphemist* - noun: one who uses euphemisms
- *euphemistic* - adjective (that describes)
- *euphemistically* - adverb (tells how)

Write *euphemism, euphemist, euphemistic,* or *euphemistically*:

3. When the realtor said that the house with doors falling off hinges only needed a few repairs, he was speaking _____.

PARTS OF SPEECH: VERBS

Circle the correct verb:

4. A. Did you (set, sit) with the Bush family during the christening?
   B. Dad always (lies, lays) with his arm over his eyes when napping.

SENTENCE COMBINING:

5. Mr. and Mrs. Hobbs attended a boat show.
   The boat show featured modestly priced houseboats.
   Mr. and Mrs. Hobbs have retired.
   Mr. and Mrs. Hobbs want to live on a houseboat.

   _____

   _____

DAY 175

CAPITALIZATION:

1. "the voyage of vasco da gama opened up trade between europe and the far east and established portuguese colonies in africa," said the historian.

PUNCTUATION:

2. This cheap brightly colored necklace said Franny is without a doubt my favorite

ANALOGIES:

Complete this analogy:

3. prairie dog : rodent :: kangaroo : _____
 (a) rat (b) marsupial (c) koala (d) Australia

PARTS OF SPEECH: PRONOUNS

Circle the correct pronoun:

4. A. The best candidate for the job is (I, me).
 B. A worker handed Cally and (I, me) free food samples.
 C. His birthday card had been signed by Tate and (we, us) girls.
 D. Have Mira and (him, he) agreed to discuss their differences?

SENTENCE COMBINING:

5. Joseph Pulitzer was penniless when he arrived in America from Budapest.
 Joseph Pulitzer was handicapped with a vision problem.
 At the time of his death, he owned two major United States newspapers.

_____

_____

DAY 176

CAPITALIZATION:

1. sir issac newton presented his light experiments before the british royal society; in 1727, he was the first scientist to be buried in westminster abbey.

PUNCTUATION:

2. Rearing up on his hind legs the stallion black and sleek jerked his head sideways

PARTS OF SPEECH: NOUNS
  Circle any proper nouns in the following sentence:

3. HER PARENTS ARRIVED AT WATERLOO STATION IN LONDON TO TAKE THE EUROSTAR THROUGH THE CHUNNEL TO PARIS.

PARTS OF SPEECH: VERBS
  Write the verb tense:

4. A. present of *to tap* - _____
   B. future of *to mow* - _____
   C. past of *to store* - _____
   D. past perfect of *to turn* - _____

SENTENCE COMBINING:

5. Madison Avenue was famous in the 1950's.
   It referred to the center of the advertising business in New York City.
   Today, it refers to the American advertising industry.

   _____
   _____

DAY 177

CAPITALIZATION:

1. in 1955, the soviet union and other communist countries created an alliance called the warsaw pact.

PUNCTUATION:

Punctuate the inside address and salutation of this business letter:

2. Morris Motors Inc
   56782 Clinton St
   Batavia NY 14020

   Dear Sir

PARTS OF SPEECH: ADVERBS

Circle the correct word:

3. He (seldom, seldomly) buys vegetables from a grocery store.

PARTS OF SPEECH: VERBS/CONJUNCTIONS

Choose the correct verb in these sentences containing correlative conjunctions. Then, circle the correlative conjunctions:

4. A. Neither the sheriff nor the deputies (has, have) found any clues.
   B. Both Conya and his brother (attend, attends) community college.
   C. Either the girls or their dad (take, takes) the car to the garage for service.

SENTENCE COMBINING:

5. Phoebe Anne Oakley Mozee set a world's record in trap shooting.
   She hit 98 out of 100 clay targets.
   She was better known as Annie Oakley.

   _____

   _____

DAY 178

CAPITALIZATION:

1. charles the great, better known as charlemagne, was the emperor of the franks who conquered saxony and established the holy roman empire.

PUNCTUATION:

2. Born in 343 B C Aristotle the Greek philosopher once said Poverty is the parent of revolution and crime

PARTS OF SPEECH: ADVERBS
   Circle any adverbs in the sentence:

3. She always plays rather quietly indoors when her mother is napping.

PARTS OF SPEECH: NOUNS
   Write a sentence containing an appositive; circle the appositive:

4. _____
   _____

SENTENCE COMBINING:

5. Cecil B. DeMille chose Hollywood for his filmaking site.
   He also had considered Flagstaff, Arizona.
   He turned down Flagstaff.
   He thought it had too many snow-topped mountains.

   _____
   _____

DAY 179

CAPITALIZATION:

1. at the cave of the apocalypse on the island of patmos is a silver band that marks where st. john wrote *revelation**.

*book of the *Bible*

PUNCTUATION:

2. Lets suppose the chairman said that youre correct Phil If that is true we have a major error in our computer network

PARTS OF SPEECH:
Circle any infinitive phrase. Write <u>S.</u> if the infinitive phrase serves as a subject, <u>D.O.</u> if it serves as a direct object, <u>P.N.</u> if it serves as a predicate nominative, and <u>APP.</u> if it serves as an appositive:

3. A. _____ She wants to be an astronaut.
   B. _____ The major company goal is to increase sales.
   C. _____ To cruise the Panama Canal has been a life-long dream.

SPELLING:
A two syllable word that ends in consonant-vowel-consonant and whose accent is on the second syllable will often double the final consonant when adding a suffix beginning with a vowel.
Example: **remit = re mit´ = re mit´ + ing = remitting**

4. A. Add *er* to *begin:* _____
   B. Add *ence* to *occur:* _____

SENTENCE COMBINING:

5. The professional volleyball player had surgery.
   The surgery revealed more extensive damage than originally thought.
   The player will miss the remainder of the season.

   _____

   _____

DAY 180

CAPITALIZATION:
Capitalize this business letter:

1.
- **(A)** 24424 north knight court
  naperville, il 60540
  december 2, 20--

- **(B)** congratulations baby gift baskets
  post office box 9999
  miami, fl 33178

- **(C)** to whom it may concern:

- **(D)** i received your victorian gift basket and loved the english teacup and saucer. is there any way that i might obtain a teapot that matches? thank you.

- **(E)** sincerely yours,
- **(F)** *Zoe Z. Horvath*
- **(G)** zoe z. horvath

PUNCTUATION:

2. John F Kennedy thirty fifth President of the U S was assassinated in Dallas Texas

DICTIONARY: GUIDE WORDS
Place a √ before a word that will appear on the same dictionary page as the words <u>liability</u> and <u>library</u>:

3. A. ___ liable   C. ___ liberty   E. ___ liasion   G. ___ libeccio
   B. ___ libel   D. ___ libration F. ___ license   H. ___ librarian

BUSINESS LETTER/ENVELOPES:
Label the parts of the business letter found in #1:

4. A. _____   E. _____
   B. _____   F. _____
   C. _____   G. _____
   D. _____

SENTENCE COMBINING:

5. In 1914, Ford Motor Company started profit sharing.
   Ten percent of the workers were not included.
   Most of this ten percent were women and boys.

_____

_____